Czechoslovakian Glass & Collectibles

Dale and Diane Barta
and
Helen M. Rose

COLLECTOR BOOKS

A Division of Schroeder Publishing Co., Inc.

The current values in this book should only be used as a guide. They are not intended to set prices, which vary greatly from one section of the country to another. Auction prices as well as dealer prices can vary greatly and are affected by condition as well as demand. Neither the Authors nor the Publisher assumes any responsibility for any losses that might be incurred as a result of consulting this guide.

Photographs by
Mr. Jan Shaw

Additional copies of this book may be ordered from:

Collector Books
P.O. Box 3009
Paducah, Kentucy 42002-3009

@ $16.95. Add $2.00 for postage and handling.

Copyright: Dale and Diane Barta, Helen M. Rose, 1992

This book or any part thereof may not be reproduced without the written consent of the Authors and Publisher.

0 1 2 3 4 5 6 7 8 9

Printed by IMAGE GRAPHICS, INC., Paducah, Kentucky

DEDICATION

Dale
For his wonderful heritage of being full Czechoslovakian.

•

Our daughter and granddaughter,
Amber
To keep her heritage alive.

•

Helen
For loving and amassing such a
beautiful collection of Czechoslovakian items.

•

Diane
For turning dreams into realization.

•

And to all the old and new collectors of Czechoslovakian items.

FOREWORD

In putting together this book in words and pictures we hope it might help a lot of collectors such as ourselves. We have found in our search of Czechoslovakian glass items there is a tremendous amount of unusual items to be found. We hope that with some of these pictures you can identify items you might otherwise pass by. Never underestimate what the Czech people have produced. We have found it helpful to read the bottom and sides of everything. You never know!

We have included a little bit of history on the glass houses and artists from the early centuries until the present.

So, on to the hunt, may you be successful in collecting some of the most beautiful glass in the world.

On The Cover

Front cover:

1. Perfume Bottle: 6" green crystal with cut base and green cut drop stopper. (Plate 25.) $155.00-160.00.

2. Purse: 8" red with black beaded web design, metal top and chain. (Plate 47.) $65.00-75.00.

3. Urn: Very unusual 15½" piece with high relief oval portraits of Isabel on one side and Phillip II on the other side, alligator head handles, matte and high gloss finishes, excellent detailing. (Not found in book.) $600.00-650.00.

4. Glass Bead Necklace: 17¼", black and white swirl beads with black beads, metal flower closure. (Plate 52.) $50.00-55.00.

Back cover:

Electric Lamp: 9½" x 6½" x 5¼", four footed brass base, design around base is done in clear and blue cut crystal beads, brass trim top covered with multi-colored glass flowers and leaves, three large cabbage roses down the center, very unique and highly collectible. (Not found in book.) $1,100.00-1,200.00.

TABLE OF CONTENTS

HISTORY OF CZECHOSLOVAKIAN GLASS

THE GLASS HOUSES

All Czechoslovakian glass had its beginning in the thirteenth and fourteenth centuries as "Bohemian Glass." All of the glass factories originally had wood furnaces and were built near forests. After the Thirty Years War (1618-1648), there was a big building boom of glass houses. A production slowdown soon occurred due to a shortage of wood to fuel the furnaces. The last factory to use wood fuel was Nova Glassworks in 1680. In 1880, there were only 169 furnaces making glass in Bohemia.

During the nineteenth century experiments were made with coal furnaces and gas generator heating systems. These systems helped quite a few factories.

All building of glassworks stopped at the beginning of the twentieth century. New factories were not built until after World War II. At that time a remote gas furnace heating system was developed. In 1965, the modern top-fired furnaces were installed. Most of the remaining factories today have modern and up-to-date facilities.

Modern glass producers in Czechoslovakia included the well-known Karlovy Vary - Moser and Skrdlovice, whose glass pieces are considered works of art. Other present manufacturers are Bohemia Glasswork, Exbor Glassworks and Zeleznobrodske.

Some of the factories and their dates are: Cribska – 1414 (closed in 1964), Falknov &

Krompoch – 1530, Mitchlovka - Skalice - Svor – 1874, Kamenicky Senov – 1886, Jilk Glassworks – 1905, Hrdina Glassworks – 1907, A Training Glassworks at Bor – 1910, Ladish (Hantich) Glassworks – 1913, Rudi Glassworks – before World War I, Vatter Factory – 1925, Hantich Glassworks annex – 1945, Karlovy Vary (Moser Factory) – 1947, New glassworks built in Novy Bor – 1965.

THE GLASS

Some of the most beautiful examples of antique glass are Bohemian. Collectors today seek the Czechoslovakian made glass pieces.

The main Bohemian crystal making centers were at Haida and Steinschonau. In 1880, the types of crystal and glass made were table crystal, crystal holloware, colored glasses, bottles and other fine ware. This was not all that was made. There were also glass pipes used for beads, glass sticks, cut glass, and colored raw glass. The quantity of Bohemian glass shipped to the United States between the years 1876 and 1880 was immense. Under the heading of "Bohemian," import records listed cut, engraved, printed, colored, painted, stained, silvered or gilded, plain, molded or pressed glass valuing $2,972,089.76.

Another important glass factory was Glatz, and in the 1920's, it had a reputation for producing exceptionally beautiful colored glass of the highest quality. The colors of amber and a fine clear red were the most decorative. Most of these pieces were done in the style and shapes of old. Many of these pieces bore a black and white sticker marked "Made in Czecho-Slovakia."

By the middle of the nineteenth century, the popularity of crystal glass waned. The Bohemian industry went from engraving on colorless glass to a new series of colored glass. An opaque series was produced, resembling basalt and red marble. Also developed was the "case technique" which provided a transparent coating on crystal. This technique enabled artisans to cut and wheel engrave. The procedure allowed a design to be cut through the top layer of crystal, allowing the colored ground crystal to show.

During this era, known as the Biedermeir Period, Bohemia had a vast supply of skilled glass engravers and cutters. These workers not only applied their skills to faceting, notching and engraving glass for their country, but also provided a steady stream of skilled laborers to work abroad. During this time, Bohemian glass dominated and its styles were imitated in many European countries and in the United States.

Another glass field is the production of excellent quality jewelry, glass beads, imitation stones and geniune garnet gemstones. It had its beginnings in the early eighteenth century and continues presently. Many of the garnets set in antique jewelry were from Bohemia, now Czechoslovakia. This was and is the specialty of Jablonec in northern Czechoslovakia.

THE ARTISTS

Some of the very well-known glassmakers and engravers came from or were trained in Czechoslovakia. One of the earliest was a glass dealer by the name Peter Hille. He came from Kreibitz, Bohemia and supplied glasses to the royal courts of Dresden in 1599 and 1610.

Casper Lehmann of Prague discovered the art and business of glass engraving and wheel engraving. From 1606 to 1608, he worked for the Elector of Savony in Dresden. In 1608, he went back to Prague and was granted the title "Imperial Gem Engraver and Glass Engraver." He was given the sole privilege of practicing the art of glass engraving within the empire in 1609. Emperor Rudolf II appointed him as the Imperial gem engraver in 1610. When Lehmann died in 1622, his privilege was inherited by his pupil, Georg Schwanhardt. Like many who learned their trade in Bohemia, Schwanhardt later returned to his native city of Nuremberg, Germany and there he founded a dynasty of glass engravers.

Ludwig Moser, 1833-1916, is probably the most noted of all Bohemian glass artists. He and his sons raised glassmaking and its production to a fine art.

A glassmaking school was founded in 1920. The Skrdlovice Glassworks, which was a combined effort of artists and glassmakers, was incorporated into the Center for Arts and Crafts in Prague. They had 28 workshops and ateliers.

Czechoslovakia has produced many great glassmakers and engravers, and artisans today are carrying on the tradition of fine excellence. These are some of the contemporary artists whose works should be considered by collectors: Jan Cerny, Pavel Hlava, Vladimir Jelinek, Ladislav Jezek, Vladimir and Zdenek Kepka, Miroslav Klinger, Stanislav Libensky, Jaroslava Brychtova-Libenska, Odrich Lipa, Lubos Metelak, Rene Roubicek, Miluce Kytkova-Roubickova, Dr. Jaromic Spacek, Jindrich Tockstein, and Bratislav Novak.

GLASS

The following types of glass are featured within this section: cased, adventurine, satin, blown cased, opaque, crystal, and colored transparent. Glassware was photographed by color to simplify identification. All measurements noted are approximate.

In the examples shown from the most expensive cased items to the less expensive single layer glass pieces, the beauty of each type of Czechoslovakian glass is apparent. The most common pieces found are varicolored, variegated and mottled glassware. These pieces can range from very subdued pastel colors to extremely bright lively colors. Some of the color combinations are very unusual but blend together beautifully. Also found are single colored pieces. These can range from pastel to very bright colors, black and a very deep ameythst. When looking for glass pieces, never rely strictly on color. Czechoslovakian glass comes in every color of the rainbow.

The decorations on glass are as varied as the glass itself. All types of decorations are incorporated on glass pieces. Depending on the piece, they can range from very elaborate enameled or painted designs to very simple designs. Some pieces have simple but elegant designs done in silver or gold. Some designs use applied serpentine or flowers and leaves made of glass applied on the piece.

Other examples are overlay pieces. These are very striking in the combination of color and design. The overlay adds just the right finishing touch to certain pieces. Adventurine glass really comes to life when placed in the light. The glitter effect from these pieces are very lovely and magical. Satin glass is as its name implies, like satin. The wonderful part of this glass is the feel of it, so soft and velvety.

Examples of decanters and glasses that range from simple to elegant are included on Plate 22. They come in all different shapes, sizes, designs and colors.

Crystal items such as salt and pepper sets, along with a boudoir clock are shown on Plate 23. Also included are a cruet, candleholder, paperweight and a clear egg-shaped paperweight with a design in the center. These are very collectible and extremely hard to find.

These are only a few examples of what can be found to collect. Whether the collector buys the most or the least expensive Czechoslovakian item, he can be assured of getting a beautifully crafted piece.

PLATE 1

Top Row: (a) Vase, 8⅜", varicolored with applied blue handles, cased; (b) Vase, 6", mottled, cased; (c) Vase, 6⅛", turquoise with mottled brown, cased; (d) Vase, 8½", cobalt blue with red overlay, cobalt base.

Middle Row: (a) Vase, 11¾", varicolored, four clear feet, cased; (b) Vase, 10", varicolored, four clear feet, cased; (c) Vase, 7¼", varicolored, applied three-foot pedestal base, cased; (d) Vase, 12", varicolored, four clear feet, cased.

Bottom Row: (a) Vase, 8", varicolored, cased; (b) Pitcher, 9", mottled colors, applied cobalt blue handle, cased; (c) Vase, 9", blue base with mottled colors, cased; (d) Vase, 7¼", varicolored, cased.

PLATE 2

Top Row: (a) Bowl, 4½", mottled colors, cased (b) Vase, 3½", mottled colors, amber cased; (c) Bowl, 4½", cream with multicolored variegated design, cased.

Middle Row: (a) Vase, 8⅜", varicolored, cased; (b) Vase, 6½", red with blue and yellow mottling, cased; (c) Bowl, 6", six-sided, mottled colors, cased; (d) Vase, 7", mottled, cased.

Bottom Row: (a) Candlestick, 8½", varicolored, cased; (b) Vase, 9½", orange with multicolored design, cased, satin finish; (c) Vase, 8¾", mottled, Jack-In-The-Pulpit design, cased; (d) Candlestick, 8½", varicolored, cased.

PLATE 3

Top Row: (a) Vase, 4¾", cobalt blue with mottled colors, cased; (b) Vase, 3½", red with mottled colors, cased; (c) Vase, 4½", variegated colors, cased; (d) Vase, 3½", varicolored, cased; (e) Vase, 4¾", cobalt blue, mottled colors, cased.

Middle Row: (a) Vase, 7", variegated, cased, satin; (b) Vase, 8", cobalt blue with mottled colors, applied handles, cased; (c) Vase, 7½", variegated colors, applied black, three footed pedestal, cased; (d) Vase, 7½", red and varicolored, cased.

Bottom Row: (a) Vase, 7", red with mottling, jet rim, cased; (b) Covered Candy, 7½", cream with mottled colors, cased; (c) Vase, 8", mottled red with jet rim and applied serpentine, cased; (d) Vase, 7", red with mottling, jet rim, cased.

PLATE 4

Top Row: (a) Vase, 4¼", mottled, metal flower arranger missing, cased; (b) Vase, 4", mottled, metal flower arranger missing, cased; (c) Vase, 4½", mottled, metal flower arranger missing, cased; (d) Vase, 4", mottled, metal flower arranger missing, cased.

Middle Row: (a) Vase, 7¼", variegated colors, cased; (b) Vase, 4⅝", varicolored, mottled, applied cobalt blue handles, cased; (c) Vase, 5½", variegated pattern, cased; (d) Vase, 6", variegated, applied jet rim on petal-shaped top, cased.

Bottom Row: (a) Vase, 6⅛", mottled, applied clear three-footed pedestal base, cased; (b) Covered Candy, 8", mottled with applied black four-footed pedestal base; (c) Vase, 6¼", mottled color, cased; (d) Covered Candy, lid missing, 8½", mottled, applied black three-footed pedestal base, cased.

PLATE 5

Top Row: (a) Vase, 8", orange with black applied serpentine design, cased; (b) Vase, 7¼", orange with black design, black applied handles, cased; (c) Vase, 8", 2 pcs., red with applied jet rim on separate jet base, cased.

Middle Row: (a) Vase, 7½", orange with ruffle top, applied flower decoration, cased; (b) Vase, 8¾", orange with silver decoration, cased; (c) Vase, 8¼", orange, mottled, cased.

Bottom Row: (a) Vase, 11¾", orange with black base, cased; (b) Vase, 11¼", dark brown base with mottling above, cased; (c) Vase, 9¾", tomato red with silver design, cased.

13

PLATE 6

Top Row: (a) Pitcher, 5", orange with applied cobalt rim and handle, tri-corner top, cased; (b) Vase, 6", orange with mottled colors, cased; (c) Mustard Pot, 4½", orange with black design, cased knob; (d) Vase, 6½", varicolored, applied cobalt three-footed pedestal base, cased.

Middle Row: (a, e) Toothpick Holder, 2¼", orange with black and green design, cased; (b) Vase, 4¾", tomato red with silver design of a lady, cased; (c) Vase, 4¼", ball design, orange with silver rim and design, cased; (d) Vase, 4¾", tomato red with silver design of a man, cased.

Bottom Row: (a) Bud Vase, 8", orange, enamel decoration; (b) Vase, 4½", orange with dark color design, cased; (c) Vase, 4¾", orange with silver rim and design, cased; (d) Vase, 4¼", orange with silver rim and design, cased; (e) Bud Vase, 8", orange with black base, cased.

14

PLATE 7

Top Row: (a) Basket, 6½", red with applied jet rim and handle, cased; (b) Mustard Pot, 5", red with black decoration and knob, cased; (c) Vase, 4¼", red with multicolored mottling on top, applied black serpentine, cased; (d) Vase, 6", red with applied cobalt blue handles, cased.

Middle Row: (a) Vase, 10", red with silver design, clear base, cased; (b) Vase, 7¾", red with mottled base, cased; (c) Vase, 5", red with black base and applied jet rim, cased; (d) Vase, 10", orange with silver design, clear base, cased.

Bottom Row: (a) Vase, 9", orange with mottled colors on base, cased; (b) Vase, 10", orange with silver rim and design, cased; (c) Vase, 8½", orange top with mottled base, cased; (d) Vase, 8½", orange mottled, applied cobalt blue handles, cased.

PLATE 8

Top Row: (a) Vase, 4", mottled colors, cased; (b) Candlestick, 3", mottled colors, cased; (c) Lamp Base, 3½", varicolored, cased, satin; (d) Vase, 4¼", varicolored, applied cobalt blue rim and ear handles, cased.

Middle Row: (a) Vase, 4¼", red and orange mottled, cased; (b) Vase, 8", orange and yellow mottled, cased; (c) Vase, 4", red and orange mottled, metal flower arranger, cased; (d) Vase, 4¼", orange with black design, cased.

Bottom Row: (a) Bud Vase, 10", yellow with silver design, clear base, cased; (b) Vase, 8⅛", orange with brown, cased; (c) Vase, 7½", varicolored, cased; (d) Vase, 10½", mottled colors, cased.

PLATE 9

Top Row: (a) Vase, 6", red with applied jet rim and applied serpentine, cased; (b) Vase, 6¾", solid red with applied cobalt blue three-footed pedestal base, cased; (c) Bud Vase, 8", black design and enameling, cased; (d) Vase, 4", red wtih three applied jet handles and rim, cased; (e) Covered Candy, 7", red with black design and knob, cased.

Middle Row: (a) Pitcher, 10⅛", red with applied jet handle, cased; (b) Vase, 11¾", red with black base, cased; (c) Vase, 8¾", red with black design, cased.

Bottom Row: (a) Vase, 7", red with applied jet rim, cased; (b) Vase, 8¼", red with jet rim and applied serpentine, cased; (c) Vase 10½", red with applied crystal and cobalt blue decoration, cased.

17

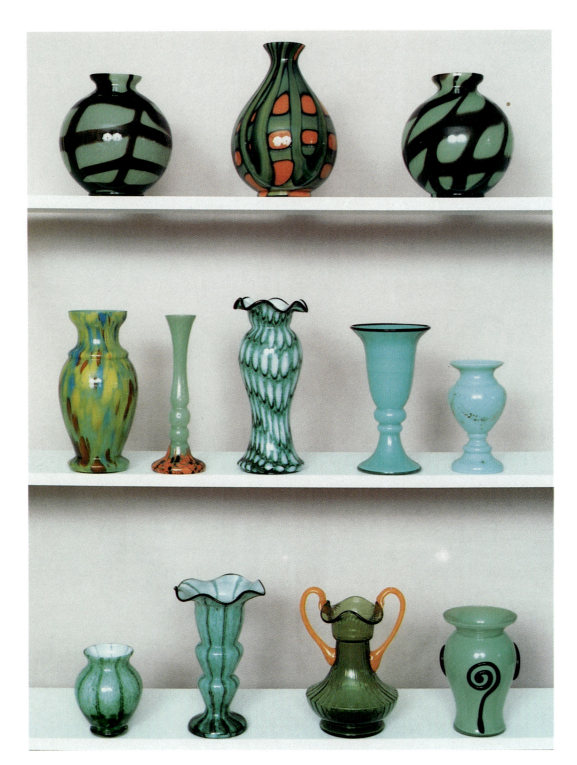

PLATE 10

Top Row: (a) Ball Vase, 6", green with brown design, cased; (b) Vase, 7½", red, green and brown design, cased; (c) Ball Vase, 6", green with brown design, cased.

Middle Row: (a) Vase, 8", mottled colors over green, cased; (b) Bud Vase, 8", green top, red and black mottled base; (c) Vase, 8⅞", white with green adventurine applied jet rim, cased; (d) Vase, 9", green with jet trim, cased; (e) Vase, 5½", pale green with gold design.

Bottom Row: (a) Vase, 4½", white with green adventurine design, cased; (b) Vase, 8", white with green adventurine, applied jet rim, cased; (c) Vase, 8", green with applied orange handles; (d) Vase, 6¼", green with applied jet design, cased.

18

PLATE 11

Top Row: (a) Vase, 8½", clear crystal with blue variegation design; (b) Vase, 6½", blue with mottled colors; (c) Vase, 7⅞", pale blue with ruffled edge, applied crystal handles, cased; (d) Vase, 8¼" ridged design, blue and white variegated, clear base with applied blue serpentine, cased.

Middle Row: (a, c) Vase, 8", blue iridescent; (b) Vase, 8½", clear crystal with variegated blue design.

Bottom Row: (a) Vase, 8¼", solid blue with applied jet rim, cased; (b) Vase, 6¾", solid blue with applied jet rim, cased; (c) Bud Vase, 8¼", blue with enamel design; (d) Vase, 6¾", pink inside, blue outside with ruffle top, cased.

PLATE 12

Top Row: (a) Vase, 7¼", black with silver rim, silver and enamel design, cased; (b) Bowl, 3¼", cobalt blue with silver rim and silver design; (c) Vase, 5", black with silver rim and silver design, cased.

Middle Row: (a, c) Candlestick, 3", black with orange interior, cased; (b) Console Bowl, 3", black with orange interior, cased.

Bottom Row: (a) Bowl, 5", black with red interior, cased; (b) Bowl, 6¼", black with orange interior, cased.

PLATE 13

Top Row: (a) Vase, 7", cobalt blue top, multi-mottled base, cased; (b, d) Bud Vase, 4", amethyst, applied gold and enamel; (c) Vase, 7", maroon with applied handles, cased; (e) Vase, 6", cobalt blue with mottled base, cased.

Middle Row: (a) Vase, 8½", amethyst with gold design; (b) Vase, 11", amethyst with silver design; (c) Vase, 10", amethyst with silver rim and design; (d) Candlestick, 8¼", jet with red ring, cased.

Bottom Row: (a) 5 pc. Berry Set (2⅛" large bowl, 1¼" small bowls), mottled color with cobalt blue applied handles, cased.

21

PLATE 14

Top Row: (a) Vase, 4¼", yellow and white mottled with metal flower arranger, cased; (b) Vase, 6¼", yellow, applied jet rim, cased; (c) Vase, 4¾", yellow, cobalt blue applied decoration, cased.

Middle Row: (a) Vase, 5¾", yellow with brown mottling base, cased; (b) Pitcher, 5", yellow with cobalt blue applied tri-cornered rim, cased; (c) Vase, 7⅞", yellow top with varicolored base, applied black serpentine, cased; (d) Vase, 6", yellow top with multi-colored mottled base, cased; (e) Vase, 5½", pink to clear with yellow variegation, bottom mottled.

Bottom Row: (a) Vase, 10", yellow with silver design, cased; (b) Vase, 8¼", solid yellow with applied jet rim, cased; (c) Vase, 13½", Jack-in-the-Pulpit design, solid yellow with applied jet rim, cased; (d) Vase, 9¼", yellow with blue applied rim and applied serpentine, cased; (e) Vase, 9", yellow, applied green decoration, cased.

22

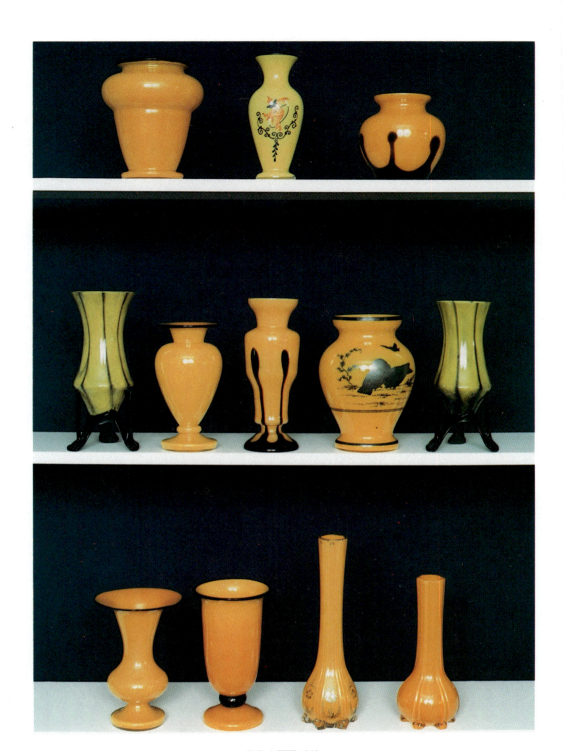

PLATE 15

Top Row: (a) Vase, 6", yellow-orange with applied jet rim, cased; (b) Vase, 6¼", yellow with clown design, applied jet rim, cased; (c) Vase, 4½", yellow-orange with brown overlay, cased.

Middle Row: (a) Vase, 8⅜", yellow and brown variegated design, applied three-footed jet pedestal base, cased; (b) Vase, 6½", yellow with applied jet rim, cased; (c) Vase, 8", orange with brown overlay, cased; (d) Vase, 7", yellow-orange with silver design, cased; (e) Vase, 7¾", yellow and brown variegated with applied three-footed jet pedestal base, cased.

Bottom Row: (a) Vase, 6¾", yellow-orange with applied jet rim, cased; (b) Vase, 7½", yellow-orange with applied jet rim and jet ring at base, cased; (c) Bud Vase, 10", yellow-orange with silver design, clear base, cased; (d) Bud Vase, 8", orange with six clear feet, cased.

PLATE 16

Top Row: (a) Ball Vase, 5", crystal, intaglio cut design; (b) Covered Candy, 7½", clear crystal with frosted and enamel design; (c) Vase, 4¾", clear crystal with mottled overlay design, intaglio cut flower design top.

Middle Row: (a) Vase, 7", frosted running horse design; (b) Vase, 12", clear and frosted with gold rim, base and decoration; (c) Vase, 9¾", clear and frosted with gold decoration.

Bottom Row: (a) Bowl, 6", white ruffled edge with maroon applied rim, cased; (b) Vase, 12½", white satin glass with gold decoration.

PLATE 17

Top Row: (a) Vase, 6½", pale green ridged top with mottled overlay bottom; (b) Vase, 9", green ridged top with mottled overlay bottom; (c) Vase, 6½", pale green ridged top with mottled overlay bottom.

Middle Row: (a) Bud Vase, 8¼", blue top and bottom with amber center; (b) Bud Vase, 11", cobalt blue base with green thorn top; (c) Vase, 7¾", pale green fan design with cobalt blue threading.

Bottom Row: (a) Vase, 8", ridged design, pale blue crystal; (b) Vase, 10", crystal with alternating frosted panels; (c) Vase, 8¾", clear crystal.

PLATE 18

Top Row: (a) Vase, 6", pink top with multicolored mottled bottom; (b) Vase, 6½", pink frosted top, blue frosted bottom, enamel design; (c) Vase, 4", clear with painted design; (d) Vase, 7", rose swirl top with multicolored mottled base.

Middle Row: (a) Vase, 6½", clear pink top with mottled bottom; (b) Bowl, 3", black with yellow interior, cased; (c) Vase, 6½", pink top with varicolored base.

Bottom Row: (a) Vase, 7", pale green with red and brown overlay, crystal; (b) Vase, 6¼", white ruffled top with pink edges, cased; (c) Vase, 5", pale green with cane and red decoration, crystal.

26

PLATE 19

Top Row: (a) Basket, 6½", blue with jet rim and clear applied handle; (b) Vase, 8¼", fan shape, mottled colors with jet rim, cased; (c) Vase, 4½", blue multicolored, cased; (d) Vase, 9", ruby glass with applied gold and enamel design.

Middle Row: (a) Vase, 4⅞", pale green with green applied handles, cased; (b) Vase, 8¼", blue green satin with hand-painted design; (c) Vase, 8", white with mottled base, applied blue serpentine, cased; (d) Vase, 6", light green with multicolors.

Bottom Row: (a) Vase, 8½", pink with white overlay design, cased; (b) Ice Bucket, 7½", crystal overshot with silver rim and handles, tongs, inside tray; (c) Ladies Cuspidor, 4", mottled colors, cased.

PLATE 20

Top Row: (a) Vase, 6", green ridged design with multicolored base; (b) Vase, 3¼", white with painted design; (c) Vase, 5", white with gold and enamel design; (d) Vase, 3¼", white with painted design; (e) Vase, 4½", frosted satin with coralene design.

Middle Row: (a) Vase, 7¾", cream color with applied aqua rim, cased; (b) Vase, 7¼", white with clear applied handles, cased; (c) Vase, 8", white with varicolored base, pale green casing.

Bottom Row: (a) Vase, 10¾", opalescent with brass ornamentation, holder; (b) Vase, 8¼", solid pink with applied jet rim, cased; (c) Vase, 10¾", opalescent with brass ornamentation, holder.

PLATE 21

Top Row: (a) Honey Pot, 5", dark blue iridescent base and lid, enamel design; (b) Glass Egg, 3", varicolored, mottled, cased; (c) Puff Box, 3½", red with black and white enameling, cased.

Middle Row: (a) Candy Jar and Lid, 7", varicolored, mottled, cobalt blue base, clear lid knob; (b) Vase, 5½", bright orange with applied cobalt blue base and side decoration, cased; (c) Vase, 5¾", varicolored, mottled, village scene and name from Czechoslovakia.

Bottom Row: (a) Mercury Ball, 4¼", possibly a candleholder; (b) Tumbler, 5", clear with green base overlay, cobalt blue threading; (c) Lamp Globe, 5½", varicolored, mottled, cased.

PLATE 22

Top Row: (a) Decanter, 10½", clear with painted design; (b) Decanter, 9", clear with enamel design; (c) Decanter, 8", clear with enamel design; (d) Shot Glasses, 2¼", clear with enamel design.

Middle Row: (a) Decanter, 8⅝", clear with enamel design; (b) Shot Glasses, 1¾", clear with enamel design; (c) Cordial Glass (one of a set of four), 3⅝", tomato red with silver design, cased; (d) Decanter, 12", tomato red with silver design, cased; (e) Seltzer Bottle, 10¾", green.

Bottom Row: (a) Decanter, 9", clear with painted green stripes; (b) Decanter, 6½", crystal ball and stopper, applied clear handle, black decoration; (c) Decanter, 5½", clear square with painted design; (d) Pitcher, 6¾", clear crystal with scene painted all around, applied handle.

PLATE 23

Top Row: (a) Salt and Pepper Set, each - 2", crystal body with porcelain duck head tops; (b) Salt Shaker, 2½", crystal cut base, black shaker top; (c) Salt and Pepper Set, each - 2¾", crystal body with porcelain hen and rooster shaker tops.

Middle Row: (a) Cruet, 6¼", crystal bottom and stopper; (b) Salt and Pepper Set, each - 2", crystal body with porcelain duck head shaker top; (c) Decanter, 6½", crystal bottom and stopper.

Bottom Row: (a) Paperweight Candleholder, 1¾", varicolored, mottled, cased, made in 1920's; (b) Paperweight, 3", multicolored in base with three pink and white striped flowers on clear stems in crystal ball; (c) Clock, 2¾", cut crystal base and top, clock works made in Waterbury, Conn.

PERFUMES AND COLOGNES

This section combines five types of glass including crystal, cut crystal, mold blown, cased and pressed. Perfumes, colognes, atomizers, puff boxes and dresser boxes are featured here. Heights and measurements are approximate.

Whether plain and simple or intricate and elaborate, each perfume bottle is a vision of everlasting beauty. Crystal, with its reflective qualities, whether clear or in colors, is beautiful to behold. Some bottles are made with cutting and polishing. This process brings the crystal to life and it sparkles like diamonds. Other bottles are done with intaglio cutting, which brings out the sharpness and detail of the design.

Cased bottles are done in the same manner as glass pieces with a variety of color combinations. They can also be of a single color with a clear crystal layer over it. These can be found on perfume and cologne bottles and atomizers.

Mold blown bottles come in a variety of shapes and sizes. Decorations range from painting a simple design to elaborate enameling with jewels. Each type of bottle is unique.

Pressed glass, especially the older pieces, still retain the sharp detail and beauty of the design. This type of glass is usually a little less expensive to purchase, but they still show the quality of good craftsmanship.

When looking for perfume bottles, the collector will find almost any size, from the very small purse size to the very large dressing table size. Decorations will vary also. Some small bottles will have extensive filigree work, enameling, and jewels on them. Some of the larger examples will be quite plain. The reverse is also found with small plain bottles and very elaborate large ones.

Colors, every combination of colors, can be found. Some colors are quite rare and hard to find. The most common bottles available are clear crystal. Usually the base will be a different color from the stopper, but some will have matching bases and stoppers. The bottle stoppers can be elaborately fashioned with the base designed plain and simple. The reverse can also be true. Whatever the combination, they will steal the heart of the viewer.

Not to be excluded are the dresser sets and boxes. These also can be found in simple to elaborate styles and in all types of glass.

The perfume bottles however are really the crowning glory of design and craftsmanship. Of all items of Czechoslovakian origin to collect, perfumes hold the greatest beauty.

PLATE 24

Top Row: (a) Cut Crystal, 6¾", clear cut base, amethyst drop stopper, intaglio cut design; (b) Cut Crystal, 4¾", clear cut base, amethyst drop stopper, intaglio cut design; (c) Crystal, 4¾", clear and frosted base, clear tree design stopper; (d) Crystal, 5½", clear cut base, clear cut design stopper; (e) Crystal, 5¾", clear cut base, clear cut stopper.

Middle Row: (a) Perfume, 3½", graduated bell shape, iridescent bottle with painted light green stripes, faceted drop stopper, top is painted green; (b) Crystal, 7", clear cut base, prism cut, clear stopper, neck of bottle has been ground down. (c) Perfume, 3½", graduated bell shape, amber iridescent bottle with painted dark blue stripes, faceted drop stopper, top is painted dark blue; (d) Crystal, 4¼", clear cut base, clear design, drop stopper; (e) Perfume, 3½", graduated bell shape, iridescent bottle with dark green stripes, faceted drop stopper, top is painted dark green.

Bottom Row: (a) Crystal, 5¾", clear cut base, clear intaglio cut drop stopper; (b) Crystal, 5½", green cut base, clear cut leaf design stopper; (c) Crystal, 6", clear cut base, pink cut drop stopper; (d) Crystal, 6½", green cut ball base, green intaglio cut drop stopper; (e) Crystal, 5¾", amber cut base, amber intaglio cut design drop stopper.

PLATE 25

Top Row: (a) Crystal, 4⅞", clear cut base, prism cut clear drop stopper; (b) Crystal, 6", green cut base, green cut drop stopper; (c) Crystal, 5½", clear and frosted satin cut base, light blue drop stopper; (d) Crystal, 3½", clear cut base, intaglio cut frosted design drop stopper.

Middle Row: (a) Perfume, 2", crystal covered with metal filigree and enamel, blue jeweled stopper; (b) Crystal, 3", green cut base with metal filigree and green jewels, green cut drop stopper; (c) Perfume, 2¼", crystal with metal filigree and jewels overall; petit point center, blue jeweled top drop stopper; (d) Crystal, 2⅜", purse size, jeweled decorated drop stopper; (e) Crystal, 2⅜", purse size, jeweled drop stopper; (f) Crystal, 2⅜", purse size, jeweled drop stopper.

Bottom Row: (a, c) Crystal, 8⅝", heavyweight; (b) Crystal, 4¼", clear cut base, red cut drop stopper.

PLATE 26

Top Row: **(a) Perfume, 3", black opaque base with jeweled decoration, black stopper; (b) Perfume, 5½", black opaque cut base and stopper; (c) Perfume, 4½", black opaque base with clear crystal stopper; (d) Perfume, 5½", black opaque base with jeweled decoration, light blue satin stopper has gold trim.**

Middle Row: **(a) Crystal , 4½", smoky cut base with transparent black stopper; (b) Crystal, 5½", blue base with intaglio cut stopper of man and woman dancing; (c) Atomizer, 4½", cobalt blue bottle with white enameling with gold trim; (d) Perfume, 3", dark blue enameling with gold trim, jewels around the neck and top, small chain, rare.**

Bottom Row: **(a) Perfume, 3½", red painted bottle with enameled design, red glass topped stopper; (b) Atomizer, 6¼", blue painted bottle with black enameling; (c) Atomizer, 7¼", cranberry glass with gold band and enameled design; (d) Atomizer, 5½", frosted satin body with enamel flower design, sets on clear amber base.**

PLATE 27

Top Row: (a) Atomizer, 3", bright orange with gold trim, cased; (b) Atomizer Bottle, 4¾", clear and frosted with gold trim design; (c) Cologne Bottle, 4½", green bottle and stopper; (d) Atomizer, 3¼", crystal, cut base.

Middle Row: (a) Perfume, 1¾", purse size, clear green cut bottle; (b) Atomizer, 6¼", clear and pink frosted bottle, enamel decoration; (c) Cologne, 6¾", opalescent bottle, pink flower with green leaves on drop stopper; (d) Perfume, 1¾", purse size, black opaque cut bottle, clear crystal drop stopper in metal screw on lid.

Bottom Row: (a) Powder Box, 2½", black top and bottom with red rose on top; (b) Atomizer Bottle, 5½", black and orange mottled bottle, black base, cased; (c) Puff Box, 3¾", orange base and lid, gold and enamel trim, clear lid knob.

PLATE 28

Top Row: 3-pc. Dresser Set – (a, c) Cologne, 5½", ridge design base, flower decorated stopper, honey beige color; (b) Puff Box, 2¼", ridge design base and lid, flower decorated center of top, honey beige color.

Middle Row: 3-pc. Dresser Set – (a, c) Cologne, 4", clear bottle and stopper with colorful enamel flower design; (b) Puff Box, 2", clear base and lid with colorful enamel flower design on lid; (c) .

Bottom Row: (a) Dresser Box, 2¼", crystal, amethyst base with clear lid; (b) Bottle, 5½", clear with red and silver applied design, possibly a barber bottle; (c) Dresser Box, 2", crystal, yellow base and lid, cut design.

UNCOMMON ITEMS

This chapter is dedicated to the hard-to-find collectibles. Some of these items might not appeal to all collectors but they find a notable position within Czechoslovakian collectibles. With a little perseverance, collectors can locate some of these items for their collections.

Within this section is a vast array of different and unusual items. Each is unique in its own right. The letter holder and basket are both done with glass beads strung in very intricate designs. The large egg-shaped beverage container is a rather unique item. It is very decorative when not in use and closed and very functional when opened. The undamaged Christmas items are becoming harder to find. The ornaments shown in their original box are a good example of their kind.

For sparkling beauty, there are crystal faceted shade pulls to dance in the sunlight in windows. Shown for collectors who enjoy firearms is an army issue rifle. This item is a rare find.

The glass animals are charming novelty items. The card holders with cameo centers are especially nice and unusual. The more common flower pot card holders are still rather unique and are reminiscent of times gone by. Their purpose was to hold a person's namecard on the dining table at a formal dinner.

Also included in this section is a very old Bible and a child's double-sided pop-up book. Among the wooden items in this chapter are children's toys and three carved pipes. Pipes can be found in all sizes, as can knives. The knives shown have celluloid covers. One knife is especially tiny.

Spoon collectors will be interested in the five spoons displayed. Each have a lovely porcelain picture in the spoon bowl. This section also shows linen towels. These are harder to find, especially marked ones.

It must be noted to doll enthusiasts that each doll shown in this chapter is dressed in their native Czechoslovakian costumes.

All heights and measurements on items are approximate.

PLATE 29

(a) Charm, 1", blue frosted glass rabbit with jewel eyes and metal collar with jewel; (b) Charm, 1", clear frosted glass bulldog with jewel eyes and metal collar with jewel; (c) Card Holder, ¾" x 2", 2 glass Scotties, 1 white, 1 blue pulling a glass wagon filled with a glass mushroom, four-leaf clover, and die, all sitting on a metal base, glass button wheels; (d) Charm, 1", green frosted glass rabbit with jewel eyes and metal collar with jewel.

PLATE 30

Letter Holder, 25½", 3-tiered, made with cardboard and fabric with glass beads used for bottom design, trim and hanger.

PLATE 31

Card Holder, 12 x 7½", single hanging basket. Design, trim, and hanger made of glass beads.

40

PLATE 32

Right: Beverage Set, 8½", egg shaped, white with enameling, coralene design, brass closure in center.

PLATE 33

Below: Inside of beverage set shown. Tray holds decanter with six shot glasses around it.

PLATE 34

Top row: Cardboard calendar holder, 10" x 10", enamel and gold painted design.

Bottom row: Pop-up Book, 8" x 10⅜", double book with *Jack and the Beanstalk* on one side and *Hop O' My Thumb* on the other, copyright 1962 Artia Praque, printed in Czechoslovakia.

PLATE 35

Top Row: (a) 9" wooden painted figure on base, possibly for a ring toss game; (b) Bible, 5", published in 1847, ivory cover with velvet spine; (c) Wooden Sailor Toy 4¼", enamel painted, slant board walker.

Bottom Row: Linen Towels, 16" x 29", (a) blue, green and orange stripes; (b) orange, brown and green stripes; (c) dark green, red-orange and brown stripes.

PLATE 36

Left: Coffee Grinder, 12" x 4½", china bean holder with wooden top, metal grinder with clear glass grounds catcher, mounted on blue board.

Right: Poppy Seed Grinder, 9" x 3½", wooden handle grinder, brass holding bowl.

PLATE 37

Top Row: Card Holders, 2¾", hold name cards on dining table, ornate gold metal base and frame, green background with glass cameo, B.C. & D.

Bottom Row: Card Holders, 2½", set of 6, clear glass pots with clear glass flowers and leaves.

PLATE 38

White Ceramic Figurines: (a, b, d) Candleholder, 4½", angel standing; (c) Figurine, 8½", mother holding child; (e) Candleholder, 3½", angel kneeling.

45

PLATE 39

Rifle, 43¼" overall length, 24" barrel, 8mm with 98 Mauser action, imprinted "Ceskoslovenska - Zbrojovka - Brno." This is an Army carbine issue and is missing bayonet. Serial #882T1–VZ24.

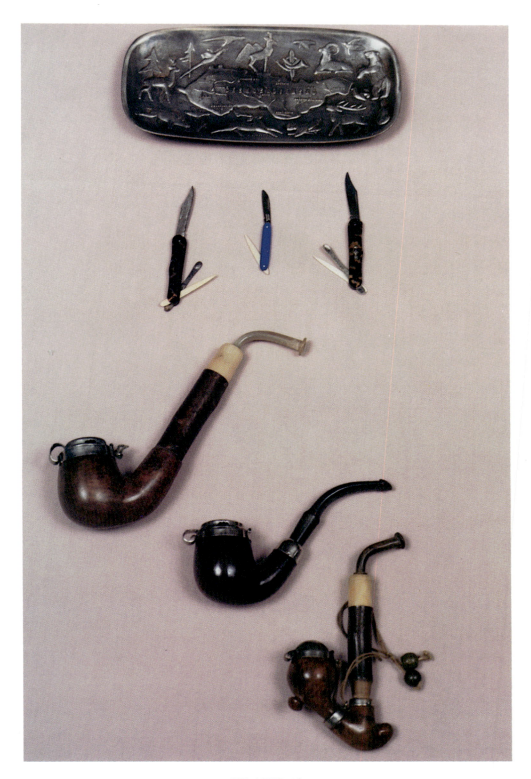

PLATE 40

Top Row: Tin Tray, 7⅞" x 3½", Czechoslovakia relief map surrounded by animals native to the country, made in Prague.

Middle Row: (a) Pocket Knife, 2¼" closed, tortise shell celluloid case with one blade, a snuff spoon, and an ivory toothpick. (b) Pocket Knife, 1½" closed – 2¼" open, blue celluloid case, one blade and one celluloid toothpick; (c) Pocket Knife, 2¼" closed, tortise shell celluloid case with one blade, a snuff spoon, and an ivory toothpick.

Bottom Row: (a) Pipe, 6¼", wood carved bowl, stainless steel bowl rim and cover; (b) Pipe, 5¼", wood carved bowl, stainless steel bowl rim and cover; (c) Mini Pipe, 5", carved wooden bowl and base, metal rim , cover and separator, decorative string ties with beads.

47

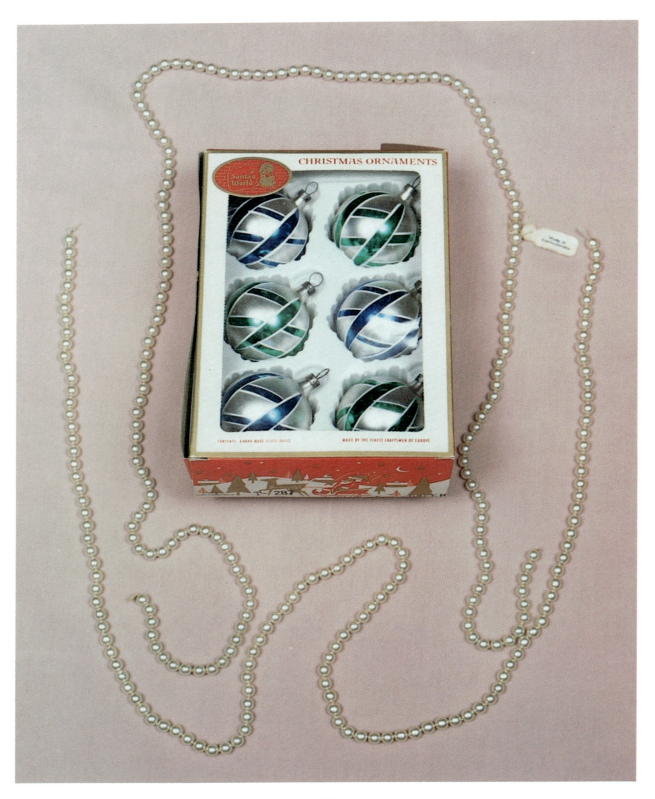

PLATE 41

Pearls: one strand is 46½" long ; the other, 53" long, used for garland on Christmas tree, individual knot between each pearl, beautifully made, necklace quality.

Glass Ornaments: set of six, 2½" each, hand made, original box. Ornaments are either bright green or blue on frosted silver with white enamel accents.

PLATE 42

Top Row: (a) Spoon, 5", fancy design handle and bowl edge, bowl center has a porcelain picture of a ballerina; (b) Spoon, 5", gold and black fancy design handle and bowl edge, bowl center has a porcelain Mona Lisa picture; (b) Spoon, 5", fancy design handle and bowl edge, bowl center has a porcelain picture of a man playing a lute.

Middle Row: Spoon, 5", fancy design handle and bowl edge, bowl center has a Blue Delft porcelain picture of windmills.

Bottom Row: Spoon, 5", gold and black fancy design handle and bowl edge, bowl center has a porcelain picture of lady reclining on a bed.

PLATE 43

Top Row: (a) Salt Shaker, 2¾", crystal, design all over, missing top; **(b)** Figurine, 4⅝", "Moses", very good detail; **(c)** Dog Figurine, 5", light gray with dark brown shading, green ears, nose, and tail, Erphila; **(d)** Salt and Pepper Set, each – 3", white pot with red stripe around top of the pot, shaker top is flower bouquet of green background with multicolored flowers; **(e)** Miniature Pitcher Vase, 3", red with white interior, raised design edge on top and bottom, fancy red handle with white accents, lady's portrait in the center.

Bottom Row: (a, d) Salt and Pepper Set, each – 2", molded petal design, base is leaf and stem, top petals have ridged design, flower center is the amber glass shaker lid; **(b)** Candy Jar and Lid, 7¾", translucent green with pedestal base, black edge on base and lid, black ring between base and body, black knob handle, multicolored flowers with green leaves and orange stems; **(c)** Candy Jar and Lid, 7½", yellow with mottled, variegated, brown design on the top and bottom, cobalt blue applied pedestal base, cased.

PLATE 44

Top Row: Dutch Girl Doll, 8" tall, blonde hair, felt material, yellow skirt with red stripe, beige shoes, blue top, orange and blue apron, white lace edge shawl, beige cap, painted face, flesh-toned arms, metal plate on foot imprinted "Czecho-slovakia, Kersa."

Bottom Row: (a) Shade Pulls, each – 4¼", amber crystal, faceted oval in the center, deep cut lines around the oval and radiating out to edges, ridged design in the lines, two blue glass beads on either side of center amber bead on top, center bead alternates strips of faceted and ridged designs, very beautifully done; (b) Mirror, 8¾" long, 3¾" diameter, 4½" handle, green crystal, intaglio cut floral vine design, regular mirror on one side, magnifying mirror on the other, foldable, gold sticker; (c) Shade Pulls, each – 4¼", amber crystal, faceted oval in the center, deep cut lines around the oval and radiating out to edges, ridged design in the lines, two black glass beads on either side of center amber bead on top, center bead alternates strips of faceted and ridged designs.

51

PLATE 45

Top Row: (a) 12" Girl Doll, plastic, dressed in native costume with headress and leather boots, one of a pair, mint in the box; (b) 12" Boy Doll, plastic, dressed in native costume with fur hat and leather boots, one of a pair, mint in the box.

Middle Row: (a) 11½" Girl Doll, dressed in native costume with kerchief, stuffed cloth body, arms, and legs, papier maché head, painted face, mohair wig; (b) 17" Boy Doll, dressed in native costume, stocking head and arms, can be a puppet or a bottle cover; (c) 12" Girl Doll, plastic, dressed in native costume, leather boots, kerchief on head, mint in the box.

Bottom Row: (a) 8" Girl doll, plastic, dressed in native costume, kerchief on head, mint in the box; (b) 5¾" Girl Doll, plastic, dressed in native costume, kerchief on head, mint in the box.

PURSES AND JEWELRY

Featured in the first half of this section are purses, handbags or evening bags. All three terms are correct. At the turn of the century most ladies carried drawstring purses. Starting in the 1920's, ladies were carrying small but flashy handbags in keeping with the fashions of the time.

The purses shown in this section are all beaded with glass beads, except one, which is made of pastel painted wooden beads. The workmanship and quality of the beads are excellent. These were definitely made to last. These lovely bags can come in many shapes, sizes and colors. The designs can be very plain and simple to very elaborate. Some have added decorations such as pearls or rhinestones. Every bag has either a zip closure, a fold-over flap, a drawstring, or a decorative metal closure. All bags also have a back strap to slide on your hand while dancing. These small bags are really full of mystery, as to who might have carried them and what places they might have gone. All of this together really make Czechoslovakian purses wonderful to collect.

The last half of this section is devoted to jewelry. Shown is a wide variety of necklaces, earrings, pins, and belt buckles. Some pieces are simple and styled for everyday wear. Others are very elaborate and for special occasions. The quality and craftsmanship of all the beads, stones, and jewels are excellent. The settings and filigree work are particularly lovely. The colors found in Czechoslovakian jewelry range from pastel shades to very bright or blended combinations. Whether demure or very bright, most pieces are very eye catching and can be real conservation pieces. The bright necklace styles shown are very similar to what is popular today.

Also shown is a variety of belt buckles. There was a time when belt buckles were a high priority fashion item. A belt buckle could really add to a simple dress and become the focal point of a fancy outfit. This can also be said of pins. The variety of buckles and pins are all unique and some are very unusual. Buckles and pins can be found in all types of materials, such as glass, metal, and even celluloid. Decorations range from plain to enameled. Others are embellished with jewels.

The pieces shown should appeal to purse and jewelry collectors alike.

PLATE 46

Top Row: Purse, 5½" x 7", pastel painted wood beads, snap closure, back hand strap.

Second Row: (a) Purse, 6½" x 8½", all beaded, background in white beads, design done in off-white and gold, metal closure top, handle done with twisted beads; (b) Purse, 6¼" x 6¾", all beaded, background done in white beads, design done in off-white and gold with pearl accents, zip top closures, beaded handles; (c) Purse, 5½" x 6⅜", all beaded, background in white beads, design done in off-white and gold plus pastels, metal closure top.

Third Row: (a) Purse, 3⅝" x 7", all beaded, background done in white beads, design done in off white and gold, fold-over flap, back hand strap; (b) Purse, 4¼" x 7", all beaded, background in white beads, design done in off-white and gold, zip top, back hand strap.

Bottom Row: Purse, 4¼" x 6⅞", all beaded, background in white beads, design done in off-white and gold plus pastels, zip top, molded beaded handle.

PLATE 47

Top Row: Purse, 4⅜" x 6⅝", all beaded bag, done completely in black beads, zip top, black hand strap.

Middle Row: (a) Purse, 3⅝" x 5⅝", all beaded bag, done completely in black beads, design done in long beads, fold-over flap, back hand strap; (b) Purse, 6½", drawstring pouch bag, back side done in red glass beads, front side done in rhinestones, crocheted drawstring top; (c) Purse, 5", round, all over beaded black bag, design done in long black beads and rhinestones, zip top, back hand strap.

Bottom Row: (a) Purse, 8", metal design closure top with chain, red material with black beaded web design, black beaded loop dangles on bottom; (b) Purse, 8", drawstring pouch bag, black material with rows of beaded dangle loops in black, silk drawstrings.

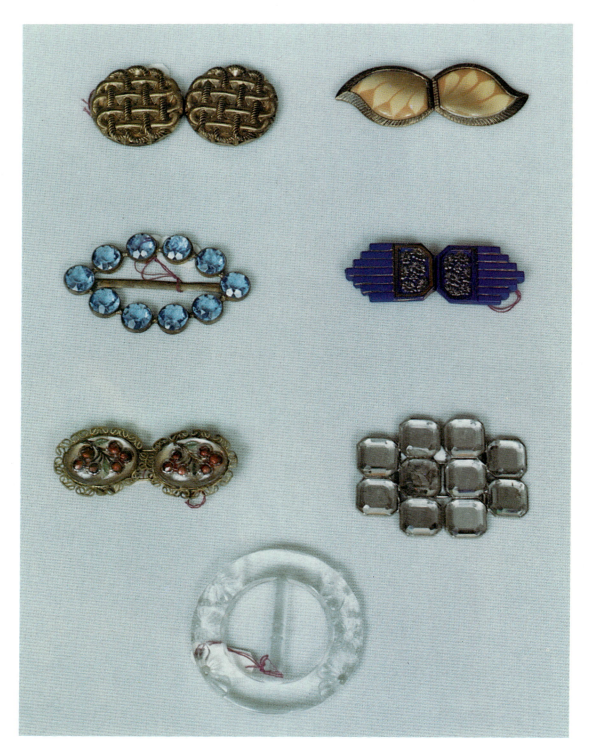

PLATE 48

Top Row: (a) Buckle, 3", belt clasps to each side, solid glass stamped and painted to look like metal; (b) Buckle, 3", belt clasps to each side, gold tone setting with light and dark tone design in celluloid in the centers.

Second Row: (a) Buckle, 2¾", gold tone setting with light blue crystals; (b) Buckle, 2¾", 2 pieces, belt clasps to each side, cobalt blue glass with gold trim.

Third Row: (a) Buckle, 2¾", 2 pieces, belt clasps to each side, gold filigree setting with cherry and leaf design in center of each side; (b) Buckle, 2½", 2 pieces, belt clasps to each side, ten large square clear glass stones.

Bottom Row: Buckle, 2½", solid one-piece glass flowers on either side.

PLATE 49

Top Row: (a) Bar Pin, 2¾", gold and enameled filigree setting, three large stones across center, six larger crystal stones and eighteen small crystal stones; **(b) Oval Cameo Pin**, gold tone with enamel setting, blue glass backing with white and ivory color glass cameo; **(c) Bar Pin, 2"**, gold tone with enamel setting, 44 small crystal stones.

Second Row: Pin, 1½", plastic, painted boy and girl in costumes; **(b) Pin, 1¾"**, gold filigree with green and white enameling, set with one large and four small white glass beads; **(c) Clip Back Pin, 1⅞"**, gold tone setting, six large oval amethyst crystals and four small amethyst crystals.

Third Row: (a) Pin, 1¼", gold tone setting, one large oval blue crystal center stone surrounded by 21 small blue crystals, unusual lock back; **(b) Clip Back Pin, 1½"**, red ridged glass with silver trim sides; **(c) Pin, 1½" diameter**, silvertone setting, set with seven larger rhinestones surrounded by 38 smaller rhinestones.

Bottom Row: (a) Six-sided Glass Pin, 1½", enamel around edge, pink center with gold trim under clear glass center; **(b) Pin, 1¾"**, silver filigree setting, set with three large blue moonstones and one small center moonstone.

57

PLATE 50

Top Row: (a) Earrings, 1¼", blue cut crystal drops, clear crystal on screw back posts; **(b) Earrings,** ¾" across, three green moonstones in center with four green crystal side stones; **(c) Earrings,** ⅞", gold tone setting, three marquis cut emerald crystals, seven round and one rectangle cut emerald crystal on each side.

Middle Row: (a) Earrings, ¾", gold filigree setting, large emerald cut crystal in center surrounded by six small light green crystals on each earring; **(b) Earrings,** 1¾", amber cut crystal drop, small chain with glass beads, dark amber stone on screw back; **(c) Earrings,** 1", gold filigree setting, set with large dark blue crystal in the center with eight small light blue crystals around the edge.

Bottom Row: (a) Earrings, ⅞", gold tone setting with three large teardrop cut emerald crystals with eight smaller round emerald crystals; **(b) Earrings,** 1", multicolored glass leaf-shaped beads with round stones in center; **(c) Earrings,** ¾", gold tone setting with one square green moonstone and two teardrops surrounded by five round green crystals.

PLATE 51

Top Row: (a) Necklace, 17", red, white, and black glass beads, metal clasp with an inset stone in the closure; (b) Necklace, 16½", green glass beads, center stones are dark green with light green beads on either side, metal clasp with green inset stone on the closure; (c) Necklace, 15", turquoise color satin beads, large center rectangle glass bead with gold trim surrounded by four-sided smaller beads, ring closure.

Bottom Row: (a) Necklace, 14", glass red and clear beads, red stone set in metal clasp closure; (b) Necklace, 15¼", yellow mottled beads, etched bead closure; (c) Necklace, 16½", crystal, amber triangle cut center stones with smaller side stones, metal filigree holders, very ornate.

PLATE 52

Top Row: (a) Necklace, 15", pink satin glass beads, one large center rectangle with gold trim surrounded by four-sided smaller beads, ring clasp; (b) Necklace, 16", flat green glass beads, metal clasp with an inset stone on the closure.

Bottom Row: (a) Necklace, 18½", yellow elongated beads, metal clasp with an inset stone on the closure; (b) Necklace, 19", orange and black beads, large center cut orange bead with two black beads on either side with two orange tear-drop shaped beads, small black and orange beads complete the necklace, filigree clasp; (c) Necklace, 17¼", glass black and white swirl beads with black beads, metal flower design closure.

60

POTTERY, PORCELAIN, AND CHINA

In this chapter Czechoslovakian pottery, porcelain and china will be detailed. To distinguish the different pottery types, a brief description is given below.

• Pottery is usually made from clay that is shaped while soft and hardened by heat.

• Porcelain is a fine white ceramic ware that is hard, translucent, sonorous, and non-porous. It is made with a single kiln firing.

• China is fired twice, once for the body and once for the glaze.

Pottery, porcelain and china can range from the more common tableware pieces to the harder to find art pottery pieces by Erphila and the Peasant Art pottery companies. The rarest pieces are by Amphora and are highly prized by collectors.

Pottery comes in all shapes and sizes. These can range from miniatures to large centerpiece items. They can be very plain and ordinary to very elaborately ornate. Whether plain or fancy, all pieces are expertly crafted. The color spectrum runs from very light pastels to very deep bright colors. The combinations of color in pottery are very different from glass, as are added decorations on pottery. They can be handpainted designs, carved designs in relief, added on flowers, even some highly unusual mottling of colors. Some pieces have a great deal of thought and imagination put into them.

Numerous pottery pieces are still available for sale. Many vases, planters, large and small pitchers, cream and sugar sets can be obtained for collections. Also available are tea sets, teapots, coffee sets, and full sets of china for the table. These collections are difficult to find intact and undamaged. Most of these items were made for daily usage. Other pottery collectibles include figurines, dresser sets, bowls of all sizes and wall pockets for holding flowers.

Matched kitchen sets or canisters are a little harder to find. The number of pieces may vary in these sets. The items stored in containers may also vary from set to set. One set may have an oatmeal container while another set will have a rice container. Not all sets are the same.

At first glance, Czechoslovakian pottery, porcelain or china pieces may be very recognizable to a collector, but other pieces may be difficult to distinguish from other types of pottery. Never assume that a piece is not "Czech." Learn to look at everything about the piece to avoid passing by a beautiful Czechoslovakian piece of pottery, porcelain, or china.

PLATE 53

Amphora Vase: 8¼", white background with cobalt blue, light blue and gold flower and leaf design, cobalt blue along top and base connecting with curved lines. Marked "R.S.K. Turn Teplitz Bohemia." Recessed mold mark - "Amphora." Manufacturer was Riessner, Stellmacher and Kessel Amphora of Turn-Teplitz, Bohemia (presently Trnovany, Czechoslovakia). All pieces by this company were made between 1892 and 1905.

PLATE 54

Top Row: (a) Vase, 10", two handled, beige color with reddish lines running all over, design in black on base and single design on top. Handle with dual holes cut out; (b) Vase, 8", beige color with reddish lines running all over, design in black on base and side wing design handles.

Bottom Row: (a) Planter, 4", beige color with reddish lines running all over, black design along upper rim and center, ear design handles on either side; (b) Vase, 8¼", beige color with reddish lines running all over, black design along base and center, square type cut out handles either side.

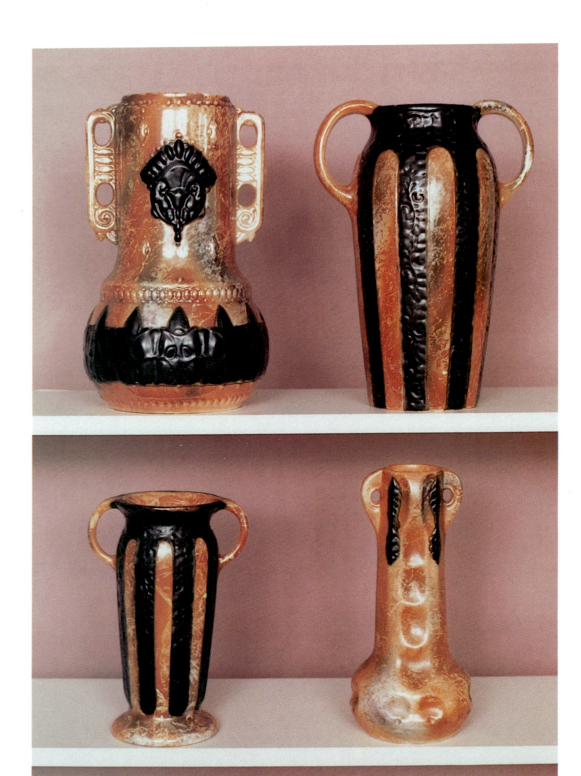

PLATE 55

Top Row: (a) Vase, 10¼", two handled, beige, black and orange mottling done with a luster type finish, black design on base and in the center, handles have double holes cut out; (b) Vase, 9½", beige, black and orange mottling, done with a luster type finish, black design along top and down sides in panels, ear type handles.

Bottom Row: (a) Vase, 8", beige, black and orange mottling, done with luster type finish, flared out base, black design along top and down sides in panels, ear type handles; (b) Vase, 9", cream, black and orange mottling, done with luster type finish, indentations down center and around base, black design near top, small ear type handles with center hole.

PLATE 56

Top Row: (a) Vase, 11¾", wedge cut design with flared base, blue ring around base, varicolored, mottled, black design along rim and stripes on sides and base; (b) Vase, 9¼", two handled, varicolored, mottled, black design along base, rim, and center design, two holes cut out in each handle.

Bottom Row: (a) Vase, 9¾", square base, multicolored, mottled, black design along base edge and just below rim, four square patches and four triangle patches done in black; (b) Bowl Vase, 4½", flared out rim, multicolored, mottled, black design along base and rim edge with teardrop design along top, middle and base.

PLATE 57

Top Row: (a) Vase, 7¾", wedge cut design with flared base, yellow, orange and black wedge design upper body, base is orange with black design and blue ring, black along top edge and base edge; (b) Pitcher, 10½", flared out top, turquoise blue mottling with reddish and cream mottling in alternating bands, double handle; (c) Pitcher, 11", Ewer type, orange mottled top and bottom with black mottling along top and bottom edge, vertical and horizontal varicolored stripes, snake shape handle.

Bottom Row: (a) Pitcher, 4", flared top, dark blue, orchid, cream and orange layered in what is called "Flame Design." Black edge on rim and black handle; (b) Pitcher, 7¼", orange, white and tan bands with multicolored design, fancy handle, black rim edge and lines. Erphila Art Pottery; (c) Vase, 7¼", sawtooth design done in orange to cream to light and dark purple, black rim edge.

PLATE 58

Top Row: (a) Leaf Salad Plate, 7", Majolica, light green and brownish yellow leaves with dark brown vine; (b) Relish Tray, 4"x 12", dark green and tan leaves with dark brown vines with light orange edges, black open handles.

Bottom Row: (a) Leaf Salad Plate, 7", Majolica, dark green and brownish yellow leaves with dark brown vine; (b) Leaf Salad Plate, 7", Majolica, tan, pale green and dark brown leaves with dark brown vine.

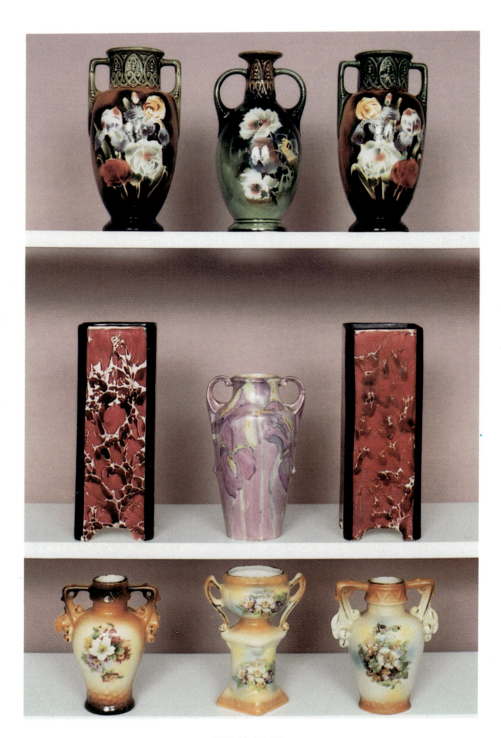

PLATE 59

Top Row: (a) Vase, 7", base dark brown with light green to tan design top with double handles, multicolored floral design in center; (b) Bud Vase, 7", light green base with light brown design blended down to dark brown, light green handles, multicolored floral design; (c) Vase, 7", base dark brown with dark green design top and handles, multicolored floral design.

Middle Row: (a) Vase, 8¼", maroon, black and white mottled design with black rim and four side corners, four raised feet; (b) Vase, 6½", orchid and cream swirled floral design and panels, two ear handles, luster finish; (c) Vase, 8¼", maroon and black with a touch of white mottling with black rim and each side corner, four raised feet.

Bottom Row: (a) Vase, 5½", dark brown base and rim, shading to rust, cream color center with multicolored floral design, two fancy handles; (b) Vase, 5½", pale orange top, center, and rim of base, yellow and cream background with multicolored florals, two side handles; (c) Vase, 5¼", rust base, rim, and top of handles, yellow and cream background with multicolored floral in the center, fancy side handles.

PLATE 60

Top Row: (a) Pitcher, 5¾", flared top, cream background with brightly colored flower design, black rim and base edge, black curved handle; (b) Vase, 6", 2 pieces, flower frog top, pale yellow bottom with raised green bow design with orchid top, orchid flower ring.

Middle Row: (a) Vase, 5", red base with black and white scroll design with multicolored center floral design; (b) Tureen, 4¼", dark blue base with black and white design around top and around multicolored floral design.

Bottom Row: (a) Pitcher, 6½", mottled yellow body, multicolored floral circle, black rim and handle; (b) Vase, 8", all-in-one vase and flower frog; green with black rim, base trim, and horizontal stripes, design is orange, yellow, and black.

PLATE 61

Top Row: (a) Coffee Mug, 4½", yellow base with very bright orange, blue, red, pink and yellow flowers, black rim and handle; Peasant Art Pottery, J. Mrazek; **(b) Lamp Base,** 12", yellow base with black rim and brightly colored flowers, upper body in orange with middle band of colorful flowers, pull chain, no shade, Peasant Art Pottery, bird on marking; **(c) Tumbler,** 4¼", black background with very bright orange, yellow, blue and pink flowers around top, Peasant Art Pottery.

Middle Row: (a) Creamer, 3¼", yellow background with black rim and handle, very bright, colorful flowers in oval, Peasant Art Pottery; **(b) Compote (fruit bowl),** 6", black base with brightly colored flowers all around, yellow center, yellow bowl with black rim and brightly colored flower band all around; **(c) Sugar Bowl with lid,** 3¾", orange background with brightly colored flowers in oval in center, black rim lid has black rim and knob with bright flowers.

Bottom Row: (a) Bowl, 2¾", orange background with black rim, three indentations along top, very bright colorful flowers along edge and coming down in V-shape, Peasant Art Pottery; **(b) Bowl,** 2½", pale blue-green background with black rim, three indentations along rim, very bright colorful flowers in oval in the center, Peasant Art Pottery.

70

PLATE 62

Top Row: (a,c) Candlesticks, 10", bright orange with flared out scalloped base, two black and white decorative bands around center, black rim around bowl and decorative lines on base; (b) Pitcher, 8¼", ram design, cream background with red and black accents. Note the ram's horn makes the handle. Erphila Art Pottery.

Bottom Row: (a) Pitcher, 4", white background with orange rim and handle, colorful orange and blue flowers with green leaf design; (b) Pitcher, 5¾", bird design, cream background with red and black accents, cream color handle, Erphila Art Pottery; (c) Pitcher, 5½", white background with purple and orange flowers with green leaves all over, orange rim and handle.

PLATE 63

Top Row: (a, c) Covered Pitcher, 8¼", white background with orange scallop rim, orange base and handle, orange flowers with green vine design, lid with vine design, orange rim with white handle. Erphila Art Pottery; (b) Pitcher, 6¼", open top, white background with orange scallop rim with orange base and handle, bright orange flowers with green vines in all over pattern, Erphila Art Pottery.

Bottom Row: (a, c) Plate, 6½", bright orange scallop rim, large orange flower in center, green vine surrounding center, Erphila Art Pottery; (b) Creamer/Pitcher, 4¼", white background with orange flowers and green vines over all, orange scallop rim, orange base and handle, Erphila Art Pottery.

PLATE 64

Top Row: (a) Coaster, 3", red with red and white single flower in center, one of a set of four; (b, d, e) Tumbler, 4¼", red with red and white design of two flowers intertwined in oval in center, one of three; (c) Pitcher, 8¼", pedestal base, black handle, red with red and white design of two intertwined flowers in oval on center of pitcher and by the rim.

Bottom Row: Pitcher, 7½", flared base, black rim, yellow background and handle, orange stripe down center of handle, tree design in orchid to cream to orange, orange base. Tumblers, set of six, 4¼", black rim with yellow background with tree design in orchid to cream to orange, orange base.

PLATE 65

Apple Set

Large Apple Bowl, 6½" high, china, all over apple design, lid has leaf design and stem handle. Small Apple Bowls, set of eight, 4⅛", china, same design as larger version.

PLATE 66

5-Piece China Tea Set

Top Row: (a) Sugar Bowl, 2¼", open style, shell design, four raised feet, white pearl luster, ear-shaped handle; (b) Tea Pot, 3½", very unusual design, looks like animal, shell design with unusual knob for lid, three raised feet, white pearl luster finish, ear-shaped handle.

Bottom Row: (a) Pitcher, 5¼", milk, shell design, single resting foot in front, curled up bottom, ear-shaped handle, white pearl luster finish; (b) Saucer for creamer, 5", shell design, white pearl luster finish; (c) Creamer, 2¼", shell design, three raised feet, ear-shaped handle, white pearl luster finish.

PLATE 67

Victoria Crown China 15-piece Coffee Service Set

(All pieces have yellow-orange luster on outside, blue-gray luster on inside.)

Top and Bottom Row: Cup and Saucer, set of six , cup - 2¼" high, saucer - 5¼" across. Black rim on saucer and cup, black cup handle.

Middle Row: (a) Creamer, 3¾", black rim and handle; (b) Coffee Pot, 9" tall, black rim on spout, pot rim, and lid rim, lid has black knob and handle; (c) Sugar Bowl, 5", black rim on bowl and lid, black knob on lid, black handles.

PLATE 68

Top Row: Dresser Box, 6½", Mans, blue center with white snow drifts on base, top with polar bear that has black and tan trim.

Middle Row: (a) Vase, 5¾" fan shape, orange with pale orange, yellow and green flower garland, design done in relief; (b) Dresser Jar and Lid, 5", orange basketweave pattern done in relief, pale orange, yellow and green flower garland design also done in relief; (c) Vase, 5¾", fan shape, orange with pale orange, yellow and green garland design in relief.

Bottom Row: (a) Basket, 4¼", dresser type, basketweave design done in relief in orange, has a green bow garland design also done in relief; (b) Dresser Box and Lid, 2½", orange basketweave design in relief with blue-green ribbon with flowers also done in relief.

PLATE 69

Top Row: (Each piece on this row has a design of bluebirds on a branch.) (a) Covered Trinket Box, 1¾", base is white with orange trim at the top and bottom; (b) Hatpin Holder, 4¾", white with orange trim around and on top; (c) Candlestick, 5¼", white with orange around and on top; (d) Trinket Box, 1¾", base is white with orange trim at the top and bottom, lid has orange rim.

Middle Row: (Each piece on this row has a white pearl lusterware finish.) (a) Dresser Tray, 11¾" x 6¼", scalloped edge; (b) Trinket Box, 1½", scalloped edge on lid and base; (c) Candlestick, 5", scalloped top and bottom edge; (d) Dresser Box, 2¾", scalloped edge on lid and base, handle knob on lid.

Bottom Row: (a) Hair Receiver, 2¾", two pieces, cream with orange trim around top and bottom of base and around edge of lid, pink and green flower design around lid and in the center of the base; (b) Trinket Box, 2¼", white pearl luster finish, gold trim, center portrait picture of man and woman on the lid; (c) Dresser Box, 2", blue with black trim, multicolored, mottled band design around base and around edge of lid, Erphila Art Pottery; (d) Trinket box, 2¼", pale orange lusterware finish overall.

PLATE 70

Top Row: (a) Pitcher, 7¾", orange top with black trim, very fancy design handle, painted design on front of a church scene with clouds and green grass; **(b)** Pitcher, 7¼", light brown spout with green handle, dark brown fading to light on the base with a floral design in the center; **(c)** Pitcher, 7¾", blue-green, fancy spout and handle, design painted in center is Bo-Peep, very decorative.

Middle Row: (a) Vase, 8", cream with pale blue edging, brown trim, high relief flowers and leaves done in pink, yellow and blue; **(b)** Vase, 8", highly decorative double handles, cream with green around top and base with brown trim, high relief applied flowers and leaves in pink and green; **(c)** Vase, 8", cream with light brown edging, dark brown top, base, trim, high relief applied flowers and leaves in pink, yellow and blue-green.

Bottom Row: (a) Vase, 5⅜", cream with pink rose and green leaf design, medium brown top, double handles, pale orange base edge; **(b)** Vase, 5¼", unusual base and handles, cream bottom with pink and green floral design in the center, deep blue-green top; **(c)** Vase, 5⅝", rust color with dark brown around top and base with double handles, vintage portrait of lady in the center; **(d)** Vase, 5⅝", cream with dark pink rose and green leaf design, dark brown top, double handles, light orange edge of bottom.

PLATE 71

Top Row: (a) Basket, 5", black handle and base, white background with green leaf vine with flower design; (b) Pitcher, 9", black edge on the top and base with black handle, white background, green leaf vine with flower design; (c) Vase, 3", white background with green leaf vine with flower design.

Bottom Row: (a, b, d) Vase, 6", white background, black edging on the top and base, dark green leaf vine and flower design, clear glaze; (c) Vase, 12½", white background, black scallop top rim, black trim on the base, green vine leaf with flower design, clear glaze; (e) Candlestick, 4½", white background, black scallop top edge and black base edge and trim, single handle, green leaf vine and flower design, clear glaze.

PLATE 72

Top Row: (a) Vase, 6¼", white background with rust and green trim at the top and bottom, painted design in the center of coach being drawn by horses; (b) Vase, 7¼", yellow shading to green pearlescent background with orange, red and green trim and design; (c) Vase, 6¾", maroon base with blue top, birds in medallion design around the top in relief.

Middle Row: (a) Vase, 9¼", blue iridescent with black rim; (b) Vase, 10", white background with orange top edge, unusual green and red side decorations, green edge around base, center design of mythical winged creatures around the center design; (c) Vase, 9½", orange mottled background with black rim, center floral design on green background.

Bottom Row: (a,e) Vase, 4½", china, white background with black stripes and rim, flower design in the center; (b, d) Vase, 4⅜", china, white background with black top, rim, and lines, black and rust artistic flower design; (c) Planter, 2⅝", indented sides, purple mottling.

PLATE 73

Top Row: (a, c) Vase, pair, 6½", white background with black trim around top and vertical lines, pink and blue flowers with green leaves in an all over design; (b) Vase, 6½", all over orange luster with black rim and black handles.

Middle Row: (a) Vase, 5¾", tan with orange luster with black rim and double black handles; (b) Vase, 5½", yellow with light orange and white pearl luster with orange rim and orange handles; (c) Vase, 5¾", pale orange luster with black rim, orange and black handles.

Bottom Row: (a) Vase, 5½", white and light gray pearl luster, black rim and black handles; (b) Vase, 5¼", very unusual, paper overlay with clear glaze, black trim on scallop rim and black handles; (c) Vase, 5½", gray pearl luster with black rim and handles.

PLATE 74

Top Row: (a) Vase, 4¾", round body, white background with black and orange trim on top, bottom and handles, multicolored floral design; (b) Vase, 4¾", red, light and dark brown mottled, variegated, all over design, handles; (c) Vase, 5⅛", white pearlescent body with black rim and base and black handles, pink and green floral design.

Middle Row: (a) Vase, 7¼", red pedestal base and top edge, black rim and black ring around base, white background with red vertical stripes, band of blue, purple and yellow flowers with green leaves, handpainted; (b) Vase, 6⅝", square design, white background with black trim around top, multicolored flower and fruit design; (c) Vase, 7½", all white, body has ridged design, note unusual curved up pedestal feet, Erphila Pottery.

Bottom Row: (a) Vase, 5¼", deep red-orange body with black trim, white cameo in the center with black silhouette of a boy and girl surrounded by a flower garland; (b) Vase, 5¼", orange lusterware finish with dark green rim at the top and base; (c) Vase, 4⅞", six sided, all red, high gloss finish.

PLATE 75

Top Row: (a) Vase, 5¼", body all done in white pearlescent finish, orange rim and handles; (b) Pitcher-style Vase, 5¾", blue top, base and handle, white center with scene, raised feet; (c) Vase, 5½", cream color luster finish with black rim and handles.

Middle Row: (a) Vase, 5⅛", royal blue body with gold trim, Old Master style picture in center; (b) Vase, 6¾", green mottled background with black rim, mosaic design in black, orange and rust; (c) Vase, 6⅛", white background with multicolored flowers, black rim.

Bottom Row: (a) Basket, 3¼", grayish background with black rim and handle, orange, yellow, black flower design; (b) Vase, 5⅛", white background with black rim, multicolored, decorative design around center; (c) Bud Vase, 4¾", pale blue pearlescent finish; (d) Basket, 3¼", purple lusterware finish.

PLATE 76

Top Row: (a) Vase, 5¼", cream base with X-design, luster finish, blue rim and handles; (b) Vase, 7½", white with ridged top, blue trim and decorative handles; (c) Vase, 5⅜", cream opalescent with pale green trim on rim, base, and handles.

Middle Row: (a)Vase, 8¼", green base done in relief design, upper body and rim done in blue-gray, green and pink flower medallions done in relief; (b) Vase, 7", opalescent body with gold rim and handles, bird design in center; (c) Vase, 7⅛", three-handled, orange center with green, yellow and black mottling on the top and bottom, dark green and blue rim, Erphila Pottery.

Bottom Row: (a) Vase, 4¼", fan design on tier base, cream background with gold trim, raised pink and green flowers and leaves; (b) Vase, 5", cream background with rust along top edge and base, side decorations are multicolored floral design; (c) Vase, 4¼", fan design with tier base, white with gold trim and blue shading along top and bottom edges, blue raised flowers and green leaves.

PLATE 77

Top Row: (a) Figurine, 5¼", white goose with gold trim and accents, high gloss glaze; (b) Planter with Figurine, 5¾", white, grape and leaf design on the planter, figure of man squeezing juice from grapes into the urn at his side, very fine detail; (c) Jam Pot, 3¾", white background with green accents on base and lid, raised fruit design with branch and leaves on front and lid; (d) Vase, 4", swan shape, white with black and orange, ceramic.

Middle Row: (a, f) Vase, 8¾", orange luster on the top and bottom, black accents, tulip flowers and leaf design, six raised feet, very ornate handles; (b, e) Cup and Saucer, cup - 1⅞", saucer - 5⁹/₁₆", white with green band, design of pale and dark orange with green, Antoinette pattern; (c) Salt and Pepper Set, each - 1¾", same design as (b); (d) Tea Pot or Creamer, 3¼", same design as (b).

Bottom Row: Pancake or Breakfast Set - (a) Pitcher, 5⅜", for syrup or cream with lid, white background with orange rim and handle, orange rim and knob on lid, multicolored flower band on pitcher and lid, very colorful; (b) Platter, 11⅜"across, same design as (a); (c) Pitcher, 7¾", for batter or milk with lid, larger version of (a).

PLATE 78

Kitchen Set

White background with blue trim, artistic design in rust, yellow, blue, light blue and orange.

Top Row: Canisters, 8¼", for coffee, rice, oatmeal, and tea.

Middle Row: (a) Cruet, 9", for oil; **(b)** Canister, 8¼", for prunes; **(c)** Salt Box, 6½" tall, wooden closure top, has hole for hanging on the wall; **(d)** Cruet, 9", for vinegar.

Bottom Row: Spice Canisters, 4", for cloves, ginger, allspice, cinnamon, mace, and nutmeg.

PLATE 79

Top Row: (a) Planter Vase, 4⅝", dark blue body with purple rim, multicolored raised fruit design on both sides, raised leaves in green, molded mark "Erphila"; (b) Basket, 5⅝", black base, handle, and rim, red dots around edge of top, green dots around edge of base, scenic oriental design around the middle.

Bottom Row: (a, c) Horse Figurine, 8", ceramic, black with turquoise mane, tail, and hooves; (b) Vase, 7¾", white, black and raspberry mottled coloring with a clear high gloss finish, registered pottery.

PLATE 80

(a) Figural Flower Frog, 5½" tall, lady with long brown hair, in a long green dress, sitting on a footed maroon frog, large yellow flower and green leaf on the side. Features on the lady are beautifully done. (b) Centerpiece Bowl, 2¼" x 10¼", bright green on the inside and top, maroon base, pink and yellow flowers with leaf design all the way around the outer rim.

PLATE 81

Top Row: (a) Pitcher, 6½", maroon background with raised fruit design, hand painted; (b) Coffee Pot, 8", lid missing, white background with blue shading along the edge, multicolored floral and bird design done in pastel colors, gold handle and trim.

Middle Row: (a) Vase, 6", peacock design, green base, blue-green body, rust, white and multicolored tail, excellent detail; (b) Bowl, 3¼", cream color with deep blue and gold banding design around bowl, picture medallion in the center.

Bottom Row: Chocolate Pot, 9½", orange lusterware finish, ear-type handle.

PLATE 82

Top Row: (a) Basket, 4¼", tomato red color with black trim, black and white decorative band around the center; (b) Basket, 4¼", orange high gloss finish with black along rim and handle edge; (c) Basket, 5", red with black base and black trim along handle, black and white floral design, registered.

Middle Row: (a) Basket, 5¾", black base, blue to beige in mottled variegated design; (b) Basket, 5¾", orange base and handle, yellow band with orange dots around bottom, dark blue, orange and green design around center.

Bottom Row: (a) Basket, 4¼", yellow with black trim along base, top rim and along handles, black and white band design; (b) Basket, 4", cream opalescent with raised braid design, orange trim; (c) Basket, 5", light orange lusterware finish.

PLATE 83

Top Row: (a) Basket, 4¼", white background of pearlescent with raised braid design, black trim along rim and handle; (b) Basket, 6", yellow background with raised design, green design with leaves across handle and pink flower on either side, four raised feet; (c) Basket, 4¼", white pearlescent luster with raised design, black trim along rim edge and handle.

Middle Row: (a) Basket, 4", cream color with raised edging design, floral design in the center; (b) Basket, 5½", cream background with green shading along edges, trim done in gold, four raised feet, floral design in the center; (c) Basket, 4¼", white glazed with raised rope design, pedestal feet, floral design in the center.

Bottom Row: (a) Basket, 4½", white opalescent with raised braid design, black trim along edges and base; (b) Basket, 5½", cream with orange shading along the top, bottom, and handle edge, floral design in the center; (c) Basket, 4", cream with pale green shading along the edges, gold trim along rim edge and handle edge, floral design in center.

PLATE 84

Top Row: (a, c) Canisters, 7½", white background with blue shading on the lid and around the top of the canister, windmill scene, raised feet, one sugar and one rice; **(b) Vinegar Cruet, 8½",** white background with blue shading on lid and neck of the bottle and the handle, same windmill scene design as (a,c).

Middle Row: Spice Canisters, 4", solid orange with black trim and lettering, for allspice, cinnamon, ginger, nutmeg; **Vinegar Cruet, 8½",** single handle, same design as canisters.

Bottom Row: (a, c) Spice Canisters, 4", round, mottled design in pink, purple and blue, opalescent base and handle, trim and lettering in gold, one for ginger and one for cloves; **(b) Sugar Canister, 5¾",** top missing, blue, green and yellow mosaic design on the bottom, blue and yellow flowers with green and orange trim around the top.

PLATE 85

Top Row: (a) Candlestick, 4", square base, white lusterware, dark blue trim; **(b)** Egg Cup, 3¾", china, white opalescent base, flower and butterfly design, blue sponge band design around the top; **(c)** Candleholder, 5⅛", saucer type attached base with wide top, ear-style handle, mauve coloring, 3 spouts on top rim; **(d)** Shaker, 5", white background with green trim and dots, for either sugar or flour.

Middle Row: (a) Pitcher, 2", miniature horse head, probably a toothpick holder, tan and white with black mane and trim; **(b)** Flower Frog, 2", orange lusterware finish with black trim; **(c)** Bank, 4⅝", black scotty dog with white accents, excellent detail; **(d)** Salt and Pepper Set, each - 2", tan ponies with dark brown mane and trim; **(e)** Miniature Vase, 2⅛", probably toothpick holder, orange lusterware finish, two handles, raised feet.

Bottom Row: (a) Toothpick Holder, 1⅞", white lusterware; **(b)** Pin Tray, 3⅛" x 5", very decorative metal holder on four raised feet, gold color, tray center is porcelain with picture of man and woman in scenic setting; **(c)** Toothpick Holder, 3½", white elephant figural design with brown eyes and green carry seat with tassels.

PLATE 86

Top Row: (a) Combination Candleholder, Match Holder, and Ashtray, 6½" x 4½", lavender center, candle bowl is purple with green trim with leaves and pink flowers, unusual item; (b) Match Holder and Ash Bowl with Attached Saucer, white background, blue flowers around edge, floral design in the center of the bowl.

Middle Row: (a) Ashtray, 4" x 2" high, solid white with dark blue anchor and white rope design; (b) Ashtray, 1½", white bowl with a ridged side piece that would hold a cigarette.

Bottom Row: Figural Man, 4", possibly a pipe holder, man has white jacket, orange and yellow pants, orange shoes, green vest, brown hair in the back, black moustache, red cheeks, black trim on face and buckle.

PLATE 87

Top Row: (a) Flower Pot, 4⅝", white background with all over multicolored flower design, gold rim, Erphila Pottery; **(b) Flower Pot**, 3½", all over turquoise color with yellow leaf design band around the top.

Middle Row: (a) Planter, 4¼", mottled brown raised design rim, dark brown top shading to gray at the bottom, 2 ring handle side decorations, four raised feet, multicolored rose design; **(b) Planter**, 4¼", brown raised design rim, decorative ring handles, four raised feet, pale blue shading to brown background with multicolored carnation design; **(c) Planter**, 4¼", mottled brown raised design rim, dark brown top shading to gray at the bottom, two ring handle decorations, four raised feet, multicolored rose design, reversed flowers from (a).

Bottom Row: (a) Covered Dish, 4¾", light brown raised basketweave design on the base, decorative ring handles, top is covered with high relief design of multicolored fruit; **(b) Bowl**, 3" high, blue, green, red and tan mottled, variegated design.

PLATE 88

Top Row: (a) Flower Arranger or Holder, 5¼", parakeet is blue and rust with black accents, sitting on light and dark colored stump; (b) Planter, 3¼", tan and yellow bird on art deco style bowl, all done in tan lusterware finish; (c) Flower Arranger or Holder, 3⅞", cream and rust colored bird sitting on a tan, brown and green circular branch; (d) Flower Arranger or Holder, 5¾", bird is rust with black accents on top and tail with multicolored wings on a pastel colored tree base.

Middle Row: (a) Flower Arranger or Holder, 5½", bird is rust with multicolors and black accents in the center of twin green branches; (b) Flower Arranger or Holder, 5½", top part is a candlestick, white pearlescent lusterware with small pastel bird on the base; (c) Flower Arranger or Holder, 5½", bird is orange, blue and gray with black accents on base of green branches; (d) Wall Pocket/Flower Holder, 7½", parrot is rust with pastel colors and brown accents sitting on a bunch of grapes.

Bottom Row: (a) Flower Arranger or Holder, 4½", woodpecker on a tree, white pearl luster with black accents, (b) Flower Arranger or Holder, 5½", bird, possibly a bird of paradise, on brown tree branch, pale blue body with multicolored long fancy tail, rust accents; (c) Flower Arranger or Holder, 4⅝", small bird on branch, rust with multicolor on bird, tan branches; (d) Wall Pocket/Flower Holder, 5⅛", fancy pale orange and white pearl luster spiral seashell with white pearl and pastel colored bird, rust colored beak.

PLATE 89

Top Row: (a) Creamer, 3½", moose head with open mouth spout, antler along rim, rust and brown color with dark brown accents, cream color antler and center of creamer, pale blue-gray base; (b) Creamer, 4½", bird with open beak spout, rust back and handle, yellow beak and front shading to cream, multicolored wings, black rim and accents; (c) Creamer, 4½", parrot, yellow front shading to cream, shading to light brown into dark brown on back and beak has dark brown accents; (d) Creamer, 4½", moose head, open mouth spout, cream color with tan, green accents along base and handle, dark brown accents.

Middle Row: (a) Creamer, 4¾", cow in sitting position, black handle, white with rust spots, open mouth spout; (b) Creamer, 4½", moose head, open mouth spout, brown with tan on moose and handle, cream color base; (c) Creamer, 3½", moose laying down, open mouth spout, dark brown to light brown shading to cream; (d) Creamer, 4½", parrot, yellow front shading to cream color, dark brown to light brown on beak, dark brown shading to light brown on back, rim and handle.

Bottom Row: (a) Creamer, 4½", parrot, orange beak and back, multicolored on wings, bird front, and handle, black accents; (b) Creamer, 4", pearl lusterware with black rim; cat handle with black spots and accents; (c) Creamer, 4½", pearl lusterware with black rim, cat handle with black spots and accents; (d) Creamer, 4½", bird, orange top, handle, and beak, yellow shading to cream on front, multicolored blue and green wings, black accents.

PLATE 90

Top Row: (a) Creamer, 3½", rust shading down to tan on the top and handle, blue design shading down to light blue-gray, lusterware finish; (b) Teapot and Lid, 4¼", same shading and finish as (a); (c) Sugar Bowl and Lid, 4¼", same shading and finish as (a).

Middle Row: (a) Teapot, 4", white pearl lusterware finish with black handle and lid top, black rim on top of spout and pot, black accent on spout; (b) Coffee Pot, 6", same finish and design as (a); (c) Sugar Bowl and Lid, 4", same finish and design as (a).

Bottom Row: (a) Creamer, 3", yellow shading to cream in the center, yellow base, gold trim on handle and rim, floral design of cabbages roses in the center; (b) Teapot and Lid, 3¾", same design and finish as (a); (c) Sugar Bowl and Lid, 3¾", same design and finish as (a).

PLATE 91

Top Row: (a) Sugar Bowl and Lid, 4¼", yellow shading to light orange to brown, raised design around bowl edge, very decorative handles; (b) Teapot and Lid, 3¾", yellow shading to light orange to brown, raised design around pot lid, camel head spout, very decorative handle; (c) Creamer, 3½", yellow shading to light orange to brown, raised design around top edge, highly decorative handle.

Middle Row: (a) Creamer, 3¼", white background, pink and green floral design in the center, gold trim along the edge, very decorative handle, scalloped edge base; (b) Sugar Bowl and Lid, 4½", white background with pink and green floral design in the center of the bowl and on the lid, gold trim on bowl rim, lid rim, and top of knob, very decorative handles, scalloped edge on base.

Bottom Row: (a) Creamer, 3½", white background with yellow center and top edge, white raised design in the center, black trim along rim edge and in between colors, black handle; (b) Covered Sugar Bowl; 4", white background with yellow center, top edge, and edge of lid, raised white design in center, black trim on rim and in between colors, black handles and black knob on lid.

PLATE 92

Top Row: (a) China Sugar Bowl, 4", open style, pink and white variegated petal design, green leaves along base, green rim, green vine handle; (b) China Creamer, 2⅞", similar shading as (a); (c) China Creamer, 3⅝", white background with raised grape and leaf design, grapes are done in lavender, leaves in green, vine handle in white; (d) China Sugar Bowl, 2⅛", open style, similar shading as (c).

Middle Row: (a) China Creamer, 2½", raised pattern all over, band design around top, gold colored, signed, hand-painted; (b) China Sugar Bowl and Lid, 2¼", coloring and pattern matches (a).

Bottom Row: (a) Creamer, 4", white background with design of man and woman with heart, done in red and green, green trim on handle, registered pottery; (b) Creamer, 4½", blue background and handle with blue and white center design of folk dancing man and woman; (c) Creamer, 3⅜", orange top and handle top, yellow base, cream color center and handle lower half, raised floral design in the center, pastel flowers with green and brown leaves.

100

PLATE 93

Top Row: (a) Creamer, 2½", white pearl lusterware finish, dark blue ear-style handle; (b) Sugar Bowl and Lid, 3½", white pearl lusterware finish, dark blue ear-style handles, dark blue open style knob on lid.

Middle Row: (a) Covered Sugar Bowl, 4", cream shading to yellow lusterware, black rim on bowl, black ear-style handles, black knob on lid; (b) Creamer, 3⅝", cream shading to yellow lusterware, black rim and black ear-style handle.

Bottom Row: (a) Creamer, 3¼", white background with black trim on the rim, handle and around the top, light and dark orange with black and green design; (b) Sugar Bowl and Lid, 3½", white background with black trim on handles, rim of bowl and edge of lid, black circle on top of knob, light and dark orange with black and green design.

PLATE 94

Top Row: (a) Sugar Bowl, 2½", open style, light orange shading to tan, petal style bowl with green rim; (b) Creamer, 3", light orange shading to tan, petal style body, green rim with green vine handle.

Middle Row: (a) Teapot, 3½", white pearl lusterware, black handle, black trim on spout, rim and open style knob on the lid; (b) Sugar Bowl with Lid, 3⅜", white pearl lusterware finish, black ear-style handles and lid handle.

Bottom Row: (a) Sugar Bowl with Lid, 4¼", tan shading to yellow lusterware finish, black ear-style handles, black rim, black knob on the lid; (b) Creamer, 3¾", tan shading to yellow lusterware finish, black handle, black rim.

PLATE 95

Top Row: (a) Creamer, 3¾", light orange base shading to cream with mottling of yellow and blue in center, orange shading along top of body and handle, pastel colored flower design in the center; **(b)** Creamer, 3⅞", dark orange along top and bottom, shading to cream in the center, handle is light and dark orange, green rim, scenic design in the center; **(c)** China Creamer, 3¼", orange luster finish with horizontal black lines around the center, black handle.

Middle Row: (a) Creamer, 3¼", white swan with black and orange accents, neck of the swan creates the handle, green pearl luster background; **(b)** China Creamer, 3⅞", white background with green rim and green accents on handle, center design of clown with dog jumping through hoop; **(c)** Creamer, 3", orange and white petal design body, green scalloped rim, green vine handle.

Bottom Row: (a) Creamer, 3¼", white background with pink, blue and yellow flowers and green leaves in all over design, gold rim, "Warwick," Erphila; **(b)** Baby Milk Pitcher, 3⅞", cream background, dark blue rim and accents on handle, three little Dutch girls on the front with "BABY" in dark blue at top, chip on rim; **(c)** Creamer, 3½", bright orange on lower half and base, white upper half and handle, orange rim.

PLATE 96

Top Row: (a) Creamer, 2½", cream color luster finish with black handle; (b) Creamer, 2½", blue-gray color, luster finish, black handle; (c) Creamer, 2¾", ball design body, bright yellow finish; (d) Creamer, 2¾", white top and handle, body is vertical stripes of gray and orange with black lines, black rim.

Middle Row: (a) Creamer, 2¾", cream color base and handle, raised design, multicolored floral top, gold rim, also accents on body and handle, "Fairfax" by Erphila; (b) Creamer, 3", blue-gray pearl luster finish, black rim; (c) Creamer, 3¼", light gray lusterware finish; (d) Creamer, 2½", pale yellow pearl luster finish with black handle and rim.

Bottom Row: (a) Creamer, 3¾", yellow and white mottled lusterware finish, black accents on handle; (b) Creamer, 3⅝", tan lusterware finish, black rim and black handle; (c) Creamer, 3¾", pale orange lusterware finish, dark green rim and handle; (d) Creamer, 3½", pale green pearl lusterware finish, bright orange handle and rim.

PLATE 97

Top Row: (a) Creamer, 3⅛", orange and white mottled lusterware finish; (b) Creamer, 3", bright red with white handle and rim, Erphila; (c) Creamer, 3", orange and white mottled lusterware finish, white handle, black rim; (d) Creamer, 3⅝", solid tan lusterware finish, black trim.

Middle Row: (a) Creamer, 3⅛", three shades of cedar wood grain design body with two black horizontal stripes around center, black rim, white handle; (b) Creamer, 4¾", white background with multicolored floral pattern, "Chelsea" by Erphila; (c) Creamer, 3", bright orange finish with black rim; (d) Creamer, 3⅝", blue color with white polka dots.

Bottom Row: (a) Creamer, 3", green color body with white polka dots, white rim, spout and handle; (b) Creamer, 3¾", tan lusterware top and base, multicolored flower band on white background around center, black handle and rim; (c) Creamer, 3⅝", brown wood barrel design with black horizontal stripes around center, black base edge and rim; (d) Creamer, 3½", tan background with black rim and handle, fruit design in blue, green and brown on front.

PLATE 98

Top Row: (a) Creamer, 4", bright red body with white handle, spout, and rim; (b) Creamer, 4⅝", background done in white in the center with orchid and black lines, orchid top, white handle and rim; (c) Creamer, 4", cream color top and bottom, cobalt blue band with gold decoration, picture in the center, gold bands above and below blue band, gold handle and rim.

Middle Row: (a) Creamer, 3", blue-gray pearl lusterware finish with black handle; (b) Creamer, 3¾", pale yellow pearlescent finish, black handle and rim; (c) Creamer, 3¾", orange and white mottled lusterware finish, black handle and rim.

Bottom Row: (a) Creamer, 3¾", pink and white horizontal bands with black lines between, white handle; (b) Creamer, 4", bright red body and handle, red interior, high gloss finish; (c) Creamer, 3½", white background with green and black horizontal stripes, green rim and base, green accents on handle, two vertical stripes of green down the center.

PLATE 99

Top Row: (a) Creamer, 4½", tri-corner spout top, purple and gray mottled background with brightly colored all over design, black handles and rim; (b) Creamer, 3¾", white background and handle, dark blue rim and stripe around base, blue and white ship design in the center; (c) Creamer, 5", bright red background and handle; brightly colored floral pattern, black rim, Coronet.

Middle Row: (a) Creamer, 5", green luster finish, black rim; (b) Creamer, 4⅝", little girl with base of dress in red, white cape and scarf with blue accents, yellow and blue rim designed like hat, flesh-toned hands and face with black, white and red accents, Erphila; (c) Creamer, 4⅛", Toby style, flesh-toned hand and face with black and red accents, yellow vest with black buttons, blue pants and tie, yellow socks and black shoes, sitting on a white base, red rim hat; (d) Creamer, 4", bright orange luster finish, black handle and rim.

Bottom Row: (a) Creamer, 4½", bright red body and handle, white interior, high gloss finish; (b) Creamer, 4", white ridged design body, brightly colored floral design, white handle and blue rim; (c) Creamer, 4½", green body and handle, white interior, high gloss finish.

107

PLATE 100

Top Row: (a) Milk Pitcher, 6¾", orange rim shading to beige, orange and beige handle, cobalt blue base, scenic design painted all around; (b) Milk Pitcher, 7¾", white background with blue shaded rim and base, handle is white in the center with top and bottom shaded blue, brightly colored shaded bubbles all over.

Middle Row: (a) Milk Pitcher, 5", tan lusterware finish with maroon and green horizontal stripes in the middle, maroon rim with white handle; (b) Milk Pitcher, 5½", wood grain design with black rim and stripe around the top.

Bottom Row: (a) China Milk Pitcher, 5⅛", pink pearl lusterware base, yellow pearl lusterware top, black stripe separating colors, black rim, black accents on the handle; (b) Milk Pitcher, 4⅞", white background with red rim, red accents on the handle with red line around the top, yellow, red, light green and dark green line design.

PLATE 101

Top Row: (a) Milk Pitcher, 4⅝", china, pink lusterware above yellow gold lusterware base, black line around the center, black rim and handle; **(b) Milk Pitcher,** 5½", tan top and handle, white background in the middle and the base, yellow gold stripes around the center, middle band is rust, white, and blue rectangles.

Middle Row: (a) Milk Pitcher, 5½", blue and white mottled pearl lusterware finish, black rim; **(b) Milk Pitcher,** 5¼", bright yellow ball design, white interior, high gloss finish.

Bottom Row: (a) Creamer, 3¼", tan top and band around top, white base and handle, middle background is white with blue, rust and white rectangles all around, black accents on design; **(b) Creamer and Sugar, Plus One,** stacked together - 4½", each piece - 1½", dark purple with black rim on the bottom set of cream and sugar, light purple with black rim on the top creamer; **(c) Creamer,** 3¾", tan rim with tan stripe around top, white base and handle, center is white with blue, maroon and white rectangles all around the middle.

PLATE 102

Top Row: (a) Mug, 3½", tan rim, top, and handle, white middle and base, separated by tan stripes, center band is rust, blue and white rectangles, black accents; (b) Mug, 2⅞", same design as (a); (c) Mini Mug, 2¼", probably from a child's set, same design as (a).

Middle Row: (a) Creamer, 3¾", tan rim and top, white center, base and handle, tan stripes around the middle, center band of blue, rust, and white rectangles with black accents; (b) Mug, 3½", tan rim and top, white center, base, and handle, tan stripes around the middle, center band of red, blue, and white rectangles with black accents; (c) Mug, 3½", same design as (a).

Bottom Row: (a) Double Salt or Nut Dish, 1⅜" tall, white with pale green edges on the petals, orange rim and handle; (b) Teapot, 4", white pearl lusterware finish with green handle, lid knob, spout, and accents; (c) Candy or Nut Basket, 3", bright orange finish with green rim and handle, white interior.

PLATE 103

Top Row: (a) Sugar Bowl and Lid, 4¼", white top and base, white handles with black trim, black trim on bowl edge, lid edge and lid knob, multicolored band design; (b) Child's Cup, 3⅛", tin base with porcelain overlay, yellow background with design of a bird and an elephant, red rim; (c) Sugar Bowl with Lid, 4", blue-gray pearl luster finish, orange rim, handles and lid knob.

Middle Row: (a) Mug, 4", tan rim, white background and handle, orchid stripe design with baroque style design in the center of each strip; (b) Mug, 3½", square body, blue-gray color around top with maroon dots, black rim and handle, colorful Oriental scene all around mug; (c) Mug, 4", tan luster around top, white background and handle, rust and orchid design all around mug, molded, divided mark.

Bottom Row: (a) Mug, 3⅝", all white including handle, dark blue and gold design with floral bouquets underneath, gold rim and accents; (b) China Cup, 2½", tan lusterware with red and blue horizontal stripes around center, probably belonging to child's tea set; (c) Sugar Bowl, 2½", open style, white background and handles, blue accent trim on handles, center design of folk man and woman dancing, design is red, white, and blue, registered; (d) Mug, 4", white background and handle, alternating horizontal rows of white with tan luster with black stripes in-between.

PLATE 104

Fine Bohemian China Pieces

White with light pastel design, gold rim

Top Row: (a) Soup Bowl, 8½"; (b) Dinner Plate, 10"; (c) Salad Plate, 7½".

Second Row: (a) Berry or Fruit Bowl, 5¼"; (b) Creamer, 3⅝", (c) Coffee Pot and Lid, 7¼"; (d) Sugar Bowl and Lid, 3⅝"; (e) Cup and Saucer, cup - 3⅛", saucer - 5⅝".

Third Row: (a) Vegetable Dish, covered, 4½" tall; (b) Dessert Plate, 6⅞"; (c) Gravy Boat with Attached Saucer, 3¾" high.

Bottom Row: (a) Platter, 12⅞"; (b) Serving Platter, 15½"; (c) Vegetable Dish, oblong, 4½" high.

PLATE 105

Top Row: (a) Soup Bowl, 2" deep, white with black and gold border design, marked "TK THUN," 1 of 4; (b) 3-Piece Gravy Set, 6½" across drip tray, 1¾" deep x 5¼" across square gravy bowl; 5¼" ladle, all done in white with a raised ridge design, E&R Inc., Erphila.

Middle Row: (a) Plate, 5¾", yellow background with blue rim edge, criss-cross border design done in black with bright orange, blue and green, large single flower design; (b) Plate, 7¼", same design as (a).

Bottom Row: (a) Creamer, 1⅝", white background and handle, orange trim on handle, multicolored border design at the top with multicolored garland of flowers in the center, probably belonging to a child's tea set; (b) Plate, 5¾", white background with brightly colored flowers in all over pattern, "Portland" pattern by Erphila; (c) Cup and Saucer, 1¾" high, white background and handle, gold edge on saucer and gold stripe around inside of cup, gold accents on handle, blue, yellow, and rust floral design in the center of cup, possibly belonging to a child's tea set, by THUN.

PLATE 106

Top Row: Bowl, 2¼", white background with red scallop design around top, row of large red dots under scallop design, row of small red dots around center, four red horizontal lines around bowl from the center to the base, Erphila; (b) Bowl, 5¾", white background with black scallop design around top, body covered with black dots all over; (c) Bowl, 1⅜", white background with red rim, red dots around top, four red horizontal lines around the bowl from center to the base.

Bottom Row: Bowl, 2", white background with green line around top edge, green dots around top, four green horizontal lines around bowl from center down to the base; (b) Bowl, 4¼", white background with green line around top edge, green dots around top, four green horizontal lines around bowl from the center down to the base.

PLATE 107

Top Row: (a) Bowl or Planter Base, 1¼" high, green high gloss glaze; **(b)** Bowl or Planter Base, 1½" high, yellow-gold lusterware.

Middle Row: (a) Flower Sprinkling Can, 6¼", green high gloss finish with raised multicolored flowers, one large and four small on each side.

Bottom Row: (a) Bowl, 2¼" high, could be a saucer, orange lusterware finish; **(b)** Bowl, 1⅜" high, could be a saucer, dark turquoise blue color with black rim.

115

PLATE 108

Top Row: Mugs, set of 4, each - 3" tall, Tom and Jerry set, white background and handle, red rim and red ring around the bottom, "Tom and Jerry" printed in red, multicolored spots all over, spots are different on each mug.

Middle and Bottom Rows: Mugs, set of 4, each - 4", tartan plaid with brown, light green, tan, red and black, tan luster handle with black accents, Erphila. (Note: each mug is just a little different from each other.)

LAMPS

This section features lamps in a variety of styles. Lamps are not a common item to find on the open market, but there are several types collectors should be aware of that might be found. The most common type of lamp to be found is electric, but some oil or kerosene lamps are still available.

Some lamps were made as a single piece while others were made as a pair. Remember it is more difficult to find a pair of lamps and they are more valuable as compared to a single lamp. Sometimes a complete Czechoslovakian made lamp will be found while others may only have the base or shade made there.

Lamps can range from very simple or plain to very decorative. Lamps can also range in size from very small dressing table size to massive chandeliers. Dressing table lamps can be highly decorated with scenes painted on them.

Another collectible find would be small perfume lamps used to scent the room. In recent years, this lamp is becoming a popular item again.

A decorative bulb cover is yet another item that is very unique. Bulb covers were slid over the bare light bulb to diffuse the light and to make the light more attractive. They are usually made of glass beads and flowers strung on wire to form a decorative pouch.

Some of the most breathtaking pieces to be seen are cut crystal chandeliers. These were very popular in most big fancy hotels and large theaters. These can be found, but they need much high space in order to hang them properly. These chandeliers are absolutely gorgeous but are also quite costly.

There are several types of beaded lamps, such as the one shown on this book cover. These are rare and extremely hard to find, making them a highly sought Czechoslovakian collectible item. The beauty and the craftsmanship are exceptional. Each lamp has its own special appeal.

All heights and measurements listed are approximate.

PLATE 109

Electric Lamp, 17" tall, very unusual shade that's beautiful when lamp is turned on, colors are mottled white, green and blue. The shade design is four-sided raised squares that come to a point in the center. The metal base has a raised leaf design around the center of the base, decorative design on the top and bottom of the base.

PLATE 110

Top Row: (a, c) Electric Vanity Lamp, 12", clear with white enameled flowers and green enameled leaves, brass top, shade has punched out design; (b) Electric Lamp, 9", rust color satin glass base and shade, hand painted and enameled design of windmills and trees.

Bottom Row: (a) Lamp Base, 5", clear with blue and white enameled flowers, brass top, probably an oil lamp; (b) Perfume Lamp, electric, 4", amethyst, criss-cross design on base, ridged design on top; (c) Light Bulb Cover, 5½", green glass flowers with red glass bead centers, brass expanding top to fit over a light bulb; (d) Lamp Base, 4½", white, yellow and blue mottled, variegated design, cased, brass top, probably an oil lamp.

PLATE 111

Lamp, 30½" tall, one of a pair. Body of the lamp is pottery with enameled colors. Design is green and white leaves with gold trim, white dots all around design. Top and bottom design is alternating stripes of white and gold around the lamp. Brass base, finial, and candlestick top with white bowl. Shade is white silk with orange and gold trim. Lamps are unmarked but brought from Czechoslovakia.

PLATE 112

Pair of Electric Lamps, each - 20½" tall, globes - 6" tall. The globes are mottled colors of red, yellow, orange, white and purple designed with small squares that come to a point in the center. Squares get smaller toward the top. The bases are metal figures of bearded men, each kneeling on one knee and wearing a toga with a fancy belt. Their arms are outstretched with flower garlands draped down each arm, across their laps and across the tops. There are large flower medallions in the garland centers. The globe holders are brass.

BOHEMIAN GLASS AND MOSER GLASS

This section of the book is to show some examples of Bohemian glass and Moser glass.

The former country of Bohemia today is one part of Czechoslovakia. Bohemian glass is considered a different branch of Czechoslovakian glass and as such deserves its own classification. Bohemian is some of the oldest Czech glass to be found.

The colors of Bohemian glass most recognizable to collectors are red cut back to amber, and red cut back to clear, but others can be found. Just a few examples are cobalt cut back to clear, shades of ameythst, and dark royal amber.

Designs are another recognizable feature of Bohemian glass. There are several designs you can find that are very common, such as deer and castle, deer and trees, deer and pine trees, florals, and animals and birds with trees. There are some designs that are not as common, such as single etchings of a clipper ship or similar designs.

Moser glass is another branch of Czechoslovakian glass that is also classified under its own heading. Moser glass was started by Ludwig Moser in 1857 in Karlsbad, Czechoslovakia, as it

is known today. Moser glass ranks with the best of Galle and Daum glass. The color and clarity of Moser glass is excellent. Most pieces are elaborately finished, some with fine gold leaf or with exceptional enameling. Moser is considered one of the premier glass engravers.

Many Moser pieces are signed while others may have a bug or insect in the design instead of a signature. Bees were one the favorite insect motifs.

When Ludwig Moser died in 1916, his two sons carried on the family business and the same quality glass was produced. The factory still produces glass and pottery today.

When looking to buy Moser glass, remember it is the most expensive of Czechoslovakian glass. Even the new Moser glass is very expensive when compared to new Czechoslovakian glass. The older Moser glass pieces are some of the finest examples of art glass to be found, but the newer pieces have their place also.

The following examples of Bohemian and Moser glass will show the collector what is available in the market. All heights and measurements are approximate.

PLATE 113

Top Row: Decanter with Matching Wine Glasses, Decanter - 15"; Wine Glasses, set of 6, - 4⅛", red base, bowl is red cut back to clear design.

Bottom Row: (a, c) Candlestick, 8½", pair, red cut back to clear design; (b) Decanter, 10", deep red cut back to clear on top and base, decanter center and stopper have clear crystal raised pattern.

PLATE 114

Top Row: (a) Ice Bucket, 5¾", red over amber, etched stag and tree design, gold trim on rim, base and handles; (b) Decanter, 15", red cut back to clear, grape and leaf design, stopper cut and designed the same way; (c) Vase, 10", red over amber, etched design of stag, gold trim on rim and base.

Bottom Row: Decanter with Matching Wine Glass, decanter - 9", wine glasses, set of 6 - 4¾", red cut back to amber, gold trim, birds flying in the design.

PLATE 115

Top Row: (a) Vase, 8½", dark royal amber base, shading to amethyst and back to royal amber, design in the glass, fluted top, amethyst applied decoration; (b) Candy Jar, 10", blue top and base, center design is cut back to clear, lid is blue, cut back to clear in the design, clear knob on the lid; (c) Vase, 9¼", dark royal amber base, shading to amethyst, design in the glass, applied amethyst rim and applied amethyst serpentine design.

Bottom Row: (a) Cruet, 7¼", red body cut back to clear in the design, applied clear handle and spout, clear ball stopper; (b) Vase, 10", red over amber, wheel cut leaf design, gold trim on the rim, top and base; (c) Decanter, 9¼", red top and base, center is frosted with red design, stopper is clear cut.

PLATE 116

Old Moser Glass

Top Row: (a) Oblong Bowl, 4½" high, blue with four clear applied feet, clear applied decoration around top and down the sides, design is done in enameling and gold; (b) Pitcher, 12", clear blue, applied gold design decoration, clear applied two-piece handle.

New Moser Glass

Bottom Row: (a, c) Wine Glasses, pair, 6¾", clear crystal, indented design all around; (b) Perfume Atomizer, 6", deep amethyst color that is almost black, gold embossed band around the lower part of the center, gold color atomizer top, silver cord and ball with silver tassel on end.

NEW GLASSWARE AND COLLECTIBLES

This chaper pertains to recent examples and some new items of Czechoslovakian glass and collectibles. There isn't much variety of new Czechoslovakian glass available in the United States. The main items imported are bells and salt and pepper sets. Other items found are decanter sets and matching patterned bowls and vases. Other than these few items, there isn't an overabundance of Czechoslovakian products to purchase. Very few places import the glassware, and pottery and art glass dealers seem nonexistant.

On a recent trip to Czechoslovakia, we brought back quite a few pieces of art glass along with some other items. The glass stores in Prague are always busy. There is quite a demand by tourists for the Czechoslovakian and Moser glass. One store had people waiting in block-long lines, and it is not unusual to wait from one to five hours to make a purchase. All types of glass and pottery are available to buy, but some are in limited supplies daily. The buyer must arrive early at the stores before their allotment for the day has been sold out. If the merchandise has been sold out, one must return the next day to try again.

Most of the art glass and crystal pieces are extremely heavy. The beautiful solid crystal paperweight we brought back weighs approximately three pounds. The colors and combination of colors in the art glass pieces are beautiful. The clear crystal items are exquisite.

The little perfume bottles as well as the glass flower pot with flowers are nicely made. These small items made and bought in Czechoslovakia have no markings or stickers on them. Several other glass pieces bought there also have no markings or stickers. Some of the larger pieces do have stickers but no marking on the glass itself.

The Moser pieces shown in the last chapter were purchased in Czechoslovakia. Although they are not as elaborate as the older Moser pieces, they are of excellent quality. The Moser glassware was marked in the glass with a signature stamp and also with a sticker.

The costume shown was very hard to acquire in Czechoslovakia and this one was located in a small town. Most people sew their own costumes and few are made for commercial sale. Costumes are worn for celebrations and festivals, such as the after harvest festival. Costumes can be made simple or elaborate, but all are colorful.

All heights and measurements for articles shown are approximate.

PLATE 117

Top Row: (a, c) Bell, pair, 7¼", red base with gold band design around the middle and gold rim, clear crystal twisted applied handle; (b) Dome-shaped Lid or Cover, 5", cranberry with white, clear crystal knob, Mary Gregory design.

Middle Row: Decanter with Matching Glasses (decanter - 13¼", glasses - 3"), blue with gold band design and gold trim.

Bottom Row: (a) Bell, 6¾", green base with gold etched design, gold band on top and rim, clear applied handle; (b) Bowl, 6½", cranberry crystal with white enameled Mary Gregory design; (c) Covered Candy Bowl, 8", green crystal, gold bands around base, gold design on the lid with gold bands around knob.

PLATE 118

Top Row: (a) Salt and Pepper with Mustard Jar, 3" tall, has glass spoon, all set on a tray, all pieces have a pattern, glass lids; (b) Shot Glass, 3¼", clear glass with enamel markings, bought in Czechoslovakia; (c) Glass, 6¼", pressed design, clear rim, small base, bought in Czechoslovakia; (d) Salt and Pepper set, each - 2¾", glass lids, all set on a glass tray, 6" across, all pieces have a design on them.

Middle Row: (a) Plate, 8", cranberry crystal, white enameled Mary Gregory design, "Mother's Day 1973"; (b) Paperweight, 3¼" tall, green design encased in clear 24% lead crystal, bought in Czechoslovakia; (c) Plate, 8", cranberry crystal, white enameled Mary Gregory design, "Christmas 1973."

Bottom Row: (a) Vase, clear glass with painted design, blue-green stripe around the top and the base; (b) Bowl, Large, 6½" high, alternating design of clear and frosted crystal, inverted bowl base, sawtooth base edge, sawtooth top rim; (c) Relish Dish, 8", half-moon shape, ridged design all the way around dish edge, design in the center of the dish.

PLATE 119

Crystal Glasses, set of six, 5⅝", pedestal base, gold rim on top, animal designs - moose, elk, wild boar, antelope, deer, and mountain sheep - in center of glass, purchased in Czechoslovakia.

PLATE 120

Top Row: (a) Free Form Bowl, 5" tall, clear crystal square indented base, top is cranberry and bottom is blue, encased in clear crystal, bought in Czechoslovakia; (b) Ashtrays, each - 3½", set of four in original box, two different designs, cut crystal; (c) Crystal Vase, free form style, 7½" tall, heather color, intaglio cut and frosted design of a bird on a branch, bought in Czechoslovakia.

Bottom Row: (a) Tumble Up (decanter - 7¾", tumbler - 3⅞"), amber red cut back to clear in the design; (b) Covered Candy Dish, 9⅞", clear base, body and lid are red cut back to clear.

PLATE 121

Top Row: (a) **Crystal Cordial Glass**, 4⅝", clear twisted stem applied to a clear amber bowl; (b) **Shallow Bowl**, 8" across, red cut back to clear, very thin glass; (c) **Bud Vase**, 9" tall, amber bubble base with clear crystal top, bought in Czechoslovakia.

Middle Row: (a, f) **Ceramic Egg Holder**, pair, 1¼", pink and white, bow design in the center, scallop design all around, bought in Czechoslovakia; (b, e) **Perfume Bottle**, pair, 2" tall, green mottled glass with black inset with a white cameo, metal lid with glass dauber, bought in Czechoslovakia; (c, d) **Miniature Basket**, pair, 2" tall, ceramic, gold and green twisted handle, multicolored flowers in the basket, gold trim on the base, flowers and handle, bought in Czechoslovakia.

Bottom Row: (a) **Knic-Knac**, 4", clear glass pot, glass flowers are pink and white with green glass leaves, green flower centers, bought in Czechoslovakia; (b, c) **Perfume Bottle**, pair, 2" tall, ridged design around the body, center is rose design with gold around it, gold lid with glass dauber, bought in Czechoslovakia; (d) **Bird Figurine**, 2¼", crystal with rainbow colors, bought in Czechoslovakia.

132

PLATE 122

Top Row: (a) Vase, 9¾", royal amber color, knobby design down the side, square design style; (b) Lamp Base, 15½" tall, white with brown lines all over, cased in clear glass, bought in Czechoslovakia.

Bottom Row: (a) Crystal Vase, free form, 12¾", green with clear cased glass, tulip edge design top, hand made, bought in Czechoslovakia; (b) Vase, 11" tall, cobalt color inside of clear cased crystal, narrow indented base, petal designed top, very heavy crystal, bought in Czechoslovakia.

PLATE 123

This Czechoslovakian outfit is usually worn for festivals and celebrations. This outfit was purchased in a small town in Czechoslovakia and brought back to the United States. It is modeled by Amber Barta. As you can see, the Czechs like brightly colored clothes as well as their colorful glassware. The red dress is a jumper style with white polka dots and has a hook and eye closure in back with wide red ribbon tie bow. The gathered skirt has wide lace and braid work at the bottom with more braid work at the hemline. The bodice has braid work all around the neckline and armholes and a large braided red, white and blue heart in the center. The white blouse is crocheted around arms and neckline with a red ribbon threaded through the crochet work at neckline, forming a bow tie. Two more red ribbons make drawstrings on arms. The apron is made of very bright multicolored woven silk brocade with a flower and leaf design and has a pink and white waistband that ties in back. Lace borders down the sides and the bottom. The hairpiece is a daisy and leaf flower band.

134

GLOSSARY

Adornment: To add on ornamentation.

Adventurine: Glass that has a glitter effect especially in the light.

Atomizer: Device used to reduce liquid to a fine spray.

Cased: To incase in a second layer. Also called double glass.

Clear Glass: No color, see through.

Coralene: Small glass beads applied and adhered to outer enamel design.

Crystal: Highest quality of glass.

Cut Glass: Glass with a design or shape obtained by cutting, grinding, and polishing.

Decoration: To add on an adornment to make an object fancier.

Drop Stopper: A long narrow glass rod with a tiny ball on the end. It is attached to the bottle top and reaches near the bottle bottom to apply perfume.

Enamel: A very shiny paint, used for design on glass surface.

Frosted: Surface of the glass is made to look frosty.

Intaglio Cut: The design is cut below the surface, giving an image in relief.

Iridescent: A rainbow play of colors on the glass surface.

Jet: A glossy dark black glass.

Mottled: A spotty or blotched design in one or more colors.

Opalescent: Milky, iridescent that has delicate changeable colors.

Opaque: Solid glass that cannot be seen through.

Ornamentation: An added detail such as metal, jewels or enameling on items.

Overlay: A decorative and contrasting design on top of a plain one.

Paint: Applied color, or to decorate with colors.

Relief: Vividness or sharpness of an outline due to contrast.

Satin Glass: Very dull finish from either being sand blasted or dipped in acid. Has a very smooth silky feel.

Serpentine: An applied design on glass in the form of a serpent or snake.

Stopper: A stubby short piece on a lid of a bottle used to apply perfume.

Varicolored: Two or more colors used in glass.

Variegated: Marks with different colors in spots, streaks or stripes.

MARKS

On the next few pages, many of the marks known to us are shown. A number of marks for glass and jewelry are very small when compared to the pottery marks. There are still more marks that we do not show. Collectors know the value difference of a piece that is marked and one that is not. But it is only fair to emphasize that some are not marked. A great majority will be marked, but some, depending on how they got here, will not be marked.

In 1887 or 1888, the United States required imported goods to be marked as to their point of origin. In the year 1921, this was changed to be more specific as to the country, such as "Nippon" which then became "Japan."

Besides exporting to our country, Czechoslovakia also exported to a great many other countries, including England. The other countries were not as stringent as to the markings of the imports, as was the United States. Many items were exported unmarked. From these countries, many pieces came to the United States by immigrants and by tourists traveling abroad. It is also good to note here that many items were sold in pairs with only one piece of the pair marked.

Some pieces made around the 1920's have no etching or stamp marks except for a sticker. This proves that some items were imported with only a sticker. Once the sticker was removed, the piece became unmarked.

Collectors need to bear in mind that not all pieces are marked and each piece must be judged on its own merit. An astute collector will know a Czechoslovakian collectible by its style even if it is not marked.

The marks below are found on pottery, porcelain, semi-porcelain and china.

The marks below are found on pottery, porcelain, semi-porcelain and china.

MADE IN CZECHOSLOVAKIA (dark green stamp) **Registered** (brown stamp)	**CZECHOSLOVAKIA** (black stamp)	 (reddish-brown stamp)

 (dark green stamp)	*Czecho-Slovakia* (reddish-orange stamp)	 CZECHOSLOVAKIA (green stamp)	VICTORIA CHINA CZECHOSLOVAKIA (black stamp)
 (dark blue-green stamp)	 (reddish-orange stamp)	 (orange stamp)	 (black stamp)
MADE IN PV CZECHOSLOVAKIA 50034 (black stamp) **Czechoslovakia** *Hand - painted* (black stamp)	 (green stamp)	 CZECHOSLOVAKIA (black stamp)	**P.A.L.T.**  (light green stamp)
 (black stamp)	 **Czechoslovakia** (black stamp)	**MZ ALTROhLAU CMR** CZECHOSLOVAKIA (green stamp)	**VICTORIA** (black stamp)

The marks below are found on pottery, porcelain, semi-porcelain and china.

(black stamp)

Eichwald
- 7023 -
Czechoslovakia

(black stamp)

(black stamp)

(black stamp)

Czechoslovakia

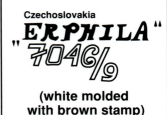

(white molded
with brown stamp)

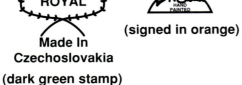

Made In
Czechoslovakia

(dark green stamp)

(signed in orange)

(white molded)

**MADE IN
CZECHOSLOVAKIA**

(blue stamp)

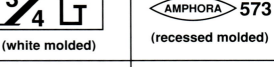

(recessed molded)

**ERPHILA
ART POTTERY**
Czecho Slovakia

(black stamp)

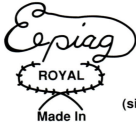

(red stamp)

(recessed molded)

(blue stamp)

(blue stamp)

(gold sticker)

(red stamp)

Czecho
Slovakia

(red stamp)

(green stamp)

CZECHOSLOVAKIA (black stamp)

LORNA
1½ L · (recessed molded)

 (black stamp)

1042 (recessed molded)
Czechoslovakia

The marks below are found on glassware, perfume bottles, and other glass items.

Made in Czecho-slovakia (black stamp)

Made in Czechoslovakia (black stamp)

Made in Czecho-slovakia (silver stamp)

CZECHO-SLOVAKIA (silver stamp)

MADE IN CZECHO-SLOVAKIA (silver stamp)

CZECHO- Made in SLOVAKIA (silver stamp)

Made in Czechoslovakia (sticker)

Made in Czecho-slovakia (sticker)

Made In Czechoslovakia (white acid etched)

CZECHO-SLOVAKIA (white acid etched)

Made in Czecho slovakia Mco Mco (black & white sticker)

MADE IN CZECHO-SLOVAKIA (white acid etched)

Made in Czecho slovakia (black & white sticker)

Made in Czecho slovakia (red & white sticker)

Czecho Slovakia (white acid etched)

Czecho Slovakia (black script stamp)

CZECHOSLOVAKIA (white acid etched)

TCHECOSLOVAQUIE (acid etched)

Czechoslovakia (white acid etched)

Moser (acid etched)

Moser MADE IN CZECHOS... (gold sticker)

CZECHOSLOVAKIA (silver stamp)

CZECHOSLOWAKIA (black stamp)

Made in Czechoslovakia (white acid etched)

Czechoslovakia (white acid etched)

The marks below are found on metal items, jewelry, and purses.

CZECHOSLOVAKIA (stamped in metal)	**MADE IN CZECHOSLOVAKIA** (molded in metal)

MADE IN CZECHO-SLOVAKIA (stamped in metal)	**CZECHO SLOVAKIA** (⬭ ⅜" metal plate)	**CZECHO** (⬭ ⅜" stamped on metal plate)	**TCHECO SLOVAQUIE** (stamped In metal)

 (stamped In metal)	**CZECHO** (stamped In metal)	**MADE IN CZECHO-SLOVAKIA** (paper label)

 (paper label in purses) black & white	 (material label in purses) black & white	**MADE IN CZECHOSLOVAKIA** (material label in purses) red & white **MADE IN CZECHOSLOVAKIA** (material label in purses) black & white

The stickers below are found on most new items from Czechoslovakia.

blue background
silver edge
silver printing

blue & gold background
red, blue, gold lettering

gold background
silver design
silver lettering

navy background
gold edge
gold lettering

gold background
blue circles
blue lettering

gold background
black edges
black lettering

silver edge
black center
silver lettering
black lettering

gold background
black lettering
black edge
gold lettering

black background
silver edge
black lettering

white background
blue moon
red circle
white columns

yellow background
black design

VALUE GUIDE

The values here reflect what is currently being quoted and asked by dealers to collectors. The values for the pieces in this book are merely here as a guide. We have tried to give a range in which the item will fall. It will depend on where you live as to what you will pay for items.

We have traveled quite a bit and talked to many dealers and collectors. We have also attended many auctions. This has helped in establishing the prices.

Czechoslovakian items are coming into their own and are attracting many more collectors.

When this happens, the pieces start getting scarce and the prices start to rise. You may find that some pieces will be either higher or lower than the range found here. As with all things, it is what the market will bear and the availability of some items in your area that will ultimately set the prices being charged.

The values in the guide are for pieces in mint condition. Remember the rarity of an item will bring into play the price set by the dealer. Remember to check items carefully. Any damage to the piece will affect the asking price.

PLATE 1
Top Row: (a) $90.00-100.00; (b) $45.00-50.00; (c) $55.00-60.00; (d) $90.00-100.00.
Middle Row: (a) $75.00-80.00; (b) $65.00-70.00; (c) $70.00-75.00; (d) $75.00-80.00.
Bottom Row: (a) $65.00-75.00; (b) $110.00-125.00; (c) $100.00-110.00; (d) $80.00-85.00.

PLATE 2
Top Row: (a) $55.00-60.00; (b) $50.00-55.00; (c) $70.00-75.00.
Middle Row: (a) $75.00-80.00; (b) $55.00-60.00; (c) $85.00-90.00; (d) $80.00-85.00.
Bottom Row: (a) $75.00-80.00; (b) $75.00-85.00; (c) $70.00-75.00; (d) $75.00-80.00.

PLATE 3
Top Row: (a) $70.00-75.00; (b) $40.00-50.00; (c) $60.00-65.00; (d) $55.00-60.00; (e) $70.00-75.00.
Middle Row: (a) $65.00-70.00; (b) $80.00-85.00; (c) $80.00-85.00; (d) $60.00-65.00.
Bottom Row: (a) $75.00-80.00; (b) $80.00-85.00; (c) $95.00-100.00; (d) $75.00-80.00.

PLATE 4
Top Row: (a) $70.00-75.00; (b) $70.00-75.00; (c) $70.00-75.00; (d) $70.00-75.00.
Middle Row: (a) $60.00-65.00; (b) $90.00-95.00; (c) $60.00-65.00; (d) $65.00-75.00.

Bottom Row: (a) $90.00-95.00; (b) $125.00-130.00; (c) $70.00-75.00; (d) $115.00-120.00.

PLATE 5
Top Row: (a) $85.00-90.00; (b) $125.00-150.00; (c) $60.00-75.00.
Middle Row: (a) $80.00-100.00; (b) $110.00-115.00; (c) $65.00-70.00.
Bottom Row: (a) $90.00-95.00; (b) $90.00-95.00; (c) $95.00-110.00.

PLATE 6
Top Row: (a) $70.00-75.00; (b) $50.00-55.00; (c) $80.00-85.00; (d) $95.00-110.00.
Middle Row: (a, e) $30.00-35.00; (b) $45.00-50.00; (c) $65.00-75.00; (d) $45.00-50.00.
Bottom Row: (a) $60.00-65.00; (b) $75.00-80.00; (c) $80.00-85.00; (d) $65.00-75.00; (e) $60.00-65.00.

PLATE 7
Top Row: (a) $75.00-80.00; (b) $85.00-90.00; (c) $90.00-95.00; (d) $90.00-95.00.
Middle Row: $60.00-65.00; (b) $65.00-70.00; (c) $70.00-75.00; (d) $60.00-65.00.
Bottom Row: (a) $65.00-70.00; (b) $110.00-115.00; (c) $80.00-85.00; (d) $80.00-90.00.

PLATE 8
Top Row: (a) $70.00-75.00; (b) $50.00-55.00; (c)

$60.00-65.00; (d) $70.00-75.00.
Middle Row: (a) $50.00-60.00; (b) $70.00-80.00; (c) $70.00-75.00; (d) $50.00-60.00.
Bottom Row: (a) $80.00-85.00; (b) $80.00-90.00; (c) $55.00-60.00; (d) $65.00-70.00.

PLATE 9

Top Row: (a) $75.00-80.00; (b) $95.00-100.00; (c) $70.00-75.00; (d) $125.00-130.00; (e) $85.00-95.00.
Middle Row: (a) $150.00-175.00; (b)$95.00-110.00; (c) $70.00-75.00.
Bottom Row: (a) 70.00-75.00; (b) $90.00-95.00; (c) $80.00-85.00.

PLATE 10

Top Row: (a) $110.00-120.00; (b) $125.00-130.00; (c) $110.00-120.00.
Middle Row: (a) $65.00-75.00; (b) $60.00-65.00; (c) $95.00-105.00; (d) $85.00-95.00; (e) $50.00-55.00.
Bottom Row: (a) $65.00-70.00; (b) $90.00-95.00; (c) $75.00-80.00; (d) $90.00-100.00.

PLATE 11

Top Row: (a) $165.00-185.00; (b) $65.00-70.00; (c) $90.00-100.00; (d) $55.00-60.00.
Middle Row: (a, c) $80.00-90.00; (b) $165.00-185.00.
Bottom Row: (a) $75.00-85.00; (b) $65.00-70.00; (c) $65.00-75.00; (d) $90.00-95.00.

PLATE 12

Top Row: (a) $140.00-145.00; (b) $60.00-70.00; (c) $90.00-95.00.
Middle Row: (Sold as set) $175.00-185.00.
Bottom Row: (a) $75.00-85.00; (b) $90.00-95.00.

PLATE 13

Top Row: (a) $65.00-70.00; (b, d) $60.00-65.00; (c) $85.00-100.00;(e) $65.00-70.00.
Middle Row: (a) $80.00-85.00; (b) $100.00-115.00; (c) $95.00-100.00; (d) $70.00-75.00.
Bottom Row: (Sold as set) $300.00-325.00.

PLATE 14

Top Row: (a) $65.00-70.00; (b) $55.00-60.00; (c) $75.00-80.00.
Middle Row: (a) $60.00-65.00; (b) $75.00-80.00; (c) $140.00-150.00; (d) $50.00-60.00; (e) $70.00-80.00.
Bottom Row: (a) $80.00-100.00; (b) $75.00-85.00; (c) $110.00-120.00; (d) $90.00-95.00; (e) $70.00-75.00.

PLATE 15

Top Row: (a) $70.00-75.00; (b) $60.00-65.00; (c) $50.00-55.00.

Middle Row: (a) $95.00-100.00; (b) $65.00-70.00; (c) $75.00-80.00; (d) $85.00-95.00; (e) $90.00-95.00.
Bottom Row: (a) $75.00-80.00; (b) $70.00-75.00; (c) $60.00-65.00; (d) $45.00-50.00.

PLATE 16

Top Row: (a) $75.00-80.00; (b) $80.00-85.00; (c) $75.00-80.00.
Middle Row: (a) $75.00-90.00; (b) $95.00-100.00; (c) $70.00-75.00.
Bottom Row: (a) $125.00-135.00; (b) $150.00-200.00.

PLATE 17

Top Row: (a) $40.00-45.00; (b) $50.00-55.00; (c) $40.00-45.00.
Middle Row: (a) $55.00-60.00; (b) $145.00-150.00; (c) $180.00-210.00.
Bottom Row: (a) $80.00-100.00; (b) $225.00-250.00; (c) $125.00-140.00.

PLATE 18

Top Row: (a) $70.00-80.00; (b) $75.00-80.00; (c) $60.00-65.00; (d) $55.00-60.00.
Middle Row: (a) $45.00-50.00; (b) $85.00-100.00; (c) $50.00-55.00.
Bottom Row: (a) $130.00-150.00; (b) $150.00-155.00; (c) $170.00-185.00.

PLATE 19

Top Row: (a) $80.00-95.00; (b) $125.00-140.00; (c) $45.00-55.00; (d) $85.00-100.00.
Middle Row: (a) $50.00-55.00; (b) $140.00-150.00; (c) $65.00-75.00; (d) $70.00-80.00.
Bottom Row: (a) $100.00-125.00; (b) $80.00-100.00; (c) $150.00-165.00.

PLATE 20

Top Row: (a) $70.00-80.00; (b) $35.00-40.00; (c) $45.00-50.00; (d) $35.00-40.00; (e) $50.00-55.00.
Middle Row: (a) $85.00-100.00; (b) 60.00-65.00; (c) $65.00-70.00.
Bottom Row: (a) $450.00-465.00; (b) $65.00-85.00; (c) $450.00-465.00.

PLATE 21

Top Row: (a) $75.00-80.00; (b) 60.00-65.00; (c) $90.00-95.00.
Middle Row: (a) $85.00-95.00; (b) $80.00-95.00; (c) $70.00-80.00.
Bottom Row: (a) $40.00-45.00; (b) $60.00-65.00; (c) $90.00-95.00.

PLATE 22

Top Row: (a) $55.00-60.00; (b) $50.00-55.00; (c) $50.00-55.00; (d) $20.00-25.00 ea.

Middle Row: (a) $50.00-55.00; (b) $20.00-25.00; (c) $30.00-35.00 ea.; (d) $95.00-110.00; (e) $100.00-125.00.

Bottom Row: (a) $50.00-55.00; (b) $90.00-95.00; (c) $45.00-50.00; (d) $165.00-175.00.

PLATE 23

Top Row: (a) $40.00-45.00; (b) $10.00-15.00; (c) $40.00-45.00.

Middle Row: (a) $55.00-60.00; (b) $40.00-45.00; (c) $55.00-60.00.

Bottom Row: (a) $40.00-50.00; (b) $145.00-150.00; (c) $95.00-110.00.

PLATE 24

Top Row: (a) $170.00-180.00; (b) $140.00-150.00; (c) $90.00-95.00; (d) $75.00-85.00; (e) $125.00-135.00.

Middle Row: (a) $160.00-180.00; (b) $85.00-95.00; (c) $160.00-180.00; (d) $85.00-90.00; (e) $160.00-180.00.

Bottom Row: (a) $140.00-155.00; (b) $95.00-105.00; (c) $165.00-175.00; (d) $150.00-165.00; (e) $125.00-135.00.

PLATE 25

Top Row: (a) $95.00-125.00; (b) $155.00-160.00; (c) $125.00-150.00; (d) $75.00-90.00.

Middle Row: (a) $80.00-85.00; (b) $80.00-85.00; (c) $50.00-65.00; (d) $50.00-75.00; (e) $50.00-75.00; (f) $50.00-75.00.

Bottom Row: (a, c) $125.00-150.00; (b) $175.00-180.00.

PLATE 26

Top Row: (a) $75.00-95.00; (b) $125.00-150.00; (c) $90.00-95.00; (d) $125.00-150.00.

Middle Row: (a) $95.00-125.00; (b) $140.00-150.00; (c) $70.00-95.00; (d) $150.00-175.00.

Bottom Row: (a) $50.00-75.00; (b) $50.00-75.00; (c) $95.00-105.00; (d) $85.00-95.00.

PLATE 27

Top Row: (a) $65.00-75.00; (b) $50.00-75.00; (c) $50.00-75.00; (d) $50.00-55.00.

Middle Row: (a) $80.00-90.00; (b) $50.00-75.00; (c) $50.00-75.00; (d) $90.00-100.00.

Bottom Row: (a) $50.00-55.00; (b) $145.00-165.00; (c) $50.00-55.00.

PLATE 28

Top Row: (a, c) $65.00-75.00; (b) $50.00-55.00.

Middle Row: (a, b, c) $25.00-40.00.

Bottom Row: (a) $50.00-55.00; (b) $40.00-45.00; (c) $55.00-60.00.

PLATE 29

(a) $25.00-35.00; (b) $25.00-35.00; (c) $30.00-35.00; (d) $25.00-35.00.

PLATE 30

$140.00-150.00.

PLATE 31

$75.00-80.00.

PLATE 32-33

$125.00-150.00.

PLATE 34

Top Row: $30.00-35.00.

Bottom Row: $40.00-45.00.

PLATE 35

Top Row: (a) $35.00-40.00; (b) $50.00-55.00; (c) $45.00-50.00.

Bottom Row: $12.00-15.00 ea.

PLATE 36

Left: $195.00-225.00

Right: $195.00-225.00.

PLATE 37

Top Row: $40.00-45.00.

Bottom Row: $12.00-15.00

PLATE 38

(a, b, d, e) $15.00-20.00; (c) $50.00-55.00;

PLATE 39

$150.00-175.00.

PLATE 40

Top Row: $40.00-45.00

Middle Row: (a) $25.00-30.00; (b) $15.00-20.00; (c) $25.00-30.00.

Bottom Row: (a) $30.00-35.00; (b) $30.00-35.00; (c) $100.00-125.00.

PLATE 41

Pearls: $25.00-35.00 pr.

Ornaments: $40.00-45.00 set.

PLATE 42
Top Row: (a) $45.00-55.00; (b) $45.00-55.00; (c) $45.00-55.00.
Middle Row: $45.00-55.00.
Bottom Row: $45.00-55.00.

PLATE 43
Top Row: (a) $12.00-15.00; (b) $30.00-35.00; (c) $45.00-50.00; (d, e) $25.00-30.00 pr.; (f) $35.00-40.00.
Bottom Row: (a, d) $30.00-35.00 pr.; (b) $80.00-85.00; (c) $80.00-85.00.

PLATE 44
Top Row: $50.00-75.00
Bottom Row: (a, c) $40.00-45.00 ea.; (b) $50.00-65.00.

PLATE 45
Top Row: (a) $110.00-120.00 pr.; (b) $110.00-120.00 pr.
Middle Row: (a) $75.00-85.00; (b) $35.00-40.00; (c) $55.00-65.00.
Bottom Row: (a) $35.00-45.00; (b) $25.00-35.00.

PLATE 46
Top Row: $40.00-45.00
Second Row: (a) $35.00-40.00; (b) $35.00-40.00; (c) $40.00-45.00.
Third Row: (a) $35.00-40.00; (b) $35.00-40.00.
Bottom Row: $40.00-45.00.

PLATE 47
Top Row: $40.00-45.00
Second Row: (a) $35.00-40.00; (b) $45.00-55.00; (c) $40.00-45.00.
Bottom Row: (a) $65.00-75.00; (b) $60.00-65.00.

PLATE 48
Top Row: (a) $20.00-25.00; (b) $20.00-25.00.
Second Row: (a) $45.00-50.00; (b) $25.00-30.00.
Third Row: (a) $40.00-45.00; (b) $25.00-30.00.
Bottom Row: $25.00-30.00.

PLATE 49
Top Row: (a) $55.00-60.00; (b) $55.00-65.00; (c) $25.00-30.00.
Second Row: (a) $25.00-30.00; (b) $40.00-45.00; (c) $50.00-55.00.
Third Row: (a) $40.00-45.00; (b) $20.00-25.00; (c) $25.00-30.00.
Bottom Row: (a) $25.00-30.00; (b) $45.00-50.00.

PLATE 50
Top Row: (a) $25.00-30.00 pr.; (b) $30.00-35.00 pr.; (c) $35.00-40.00 pr.

Middle Row: (a) $25.00-30.00 pr.; (b) $30.00-35.00 pr.; (c) $35.00-40.00 pr.
Bottom Row: (a) $35.00-40.00 pr.; (b) $20.00-25.00 pr.; (c) $30.00-35.00 pr.

PLATE 51
Top Row: (a) $40.00-45.00; (b) $30.00-35.00; (c) $40.00-45.00.
Bottom Row: (a) $35.00-45.00; (b) $40.00-45.00; (c) $75.00-80.00.

PLATE 52
Top Row: (a) $40.00-45.00; (b) $35.00-40.00.
Bottom Row: (a) $30.00-35.00; (b) $40.00-45.00; (c) $50.00-55.00.

PLATE 53
$250.00-275.00

PLATE 54
Top Row: (a) $95.00-105.00; (b) $90.00-95.00.
Bottom Row: (a) $55.00-60.00; (b) $60.00-65.00.

PLATE 55
Top Row: (a) $95.00-105.00; (b) $90.00-95.00.
Bottom Row: (a) $85.00-90.00; (b) $80.00-85.00.

PLATE 56
Top Row: (a) $110.00-115.00; (b) $90.00-95.00.
Bottom Row: (a) $85.00-90.00; (b) $80.00-85.00.

PLATE 57
Top Row: (a) $90.00-95.00; (b) $165.00-175.00; (c) $150.00-160.00.
Bottom Row: (a) $140.00-145.00; (b) $95.00-105.00; (c) $120.00-130.00.

PLATE 58
Top Row: (a) $40.00-50.00; (b) $50.00-65.00.
Bottom Row: (a) $40.00-50.00; (b) $40.00-50.00.

PLATE 59
Top Row: (a) $50.00-55.00; (b) $50.00-55.00; (c) $50.00-55.00.
Middle Row: (a) $40.00-45.00; (b) $50.00-55.00; (c) $40.00-45.00.
Bottom Row: (a) $45.00-50.00; (b) $40.00-45.00; (c) $45.00-50.00.

PLATE 60
Top Row: (a) $55.00-60.00; (b) $50.00-65.00.
Middle Row: (a) $45.00-50.00; (b) $45.00-50.00.
Bottom Row: (a) $45.00-50.00; (b) $70.00-85.00.

PLATE 61
Top Row: (a) $45.00-50.00; (b) $600.00-650.00; (c) $50.00-55.00.
Middle Row: (a) $60.00-65.00; (b) $100.00-125.00; (c) $65.00-70.00.
Bottom Row: (a) $55.00-60.00; (b) $55.00-60.00.

PLATE 62
Top Row: (a, c) $60.00-65.00; (b) $165.00-185.00.
Bottom Row: (a) $40.00-45.00; (b) $85.00-90.00; (c) $45.00-50.00.

PLATE 63
Top Row: (a, c) $75.00-80.00; (b) $65.00-70.00.
Bottom Row: (a, c) $35.00-40.00; (b) $40.00-45.00.

PLATE 64
Top Row: (a) $20.00-25.00 ea.; (b, d, e) $30.00-35.00; (c) $75.00-80.00.
Bottom Row: Pitcher: $70.00-75.00; Tumblers: $30.00-35.00 ea.

PLATE 65
Large Apple Bowl: $75.00-80.00
Small Apple Bowl: $30.00-35.00 ea.

PLATE 66
Top Row: (a) $50.00-55.00; (b) $90.00-95.00.
Bottom Row: (a) $70.00-75.00; (b) $35.00-40.00; (c) $50.00-55.00.

PLATE 67
Top Row: Cups and Saucers: $15.00-20.00 ea.
Middle Row: (a) $35.00-40.00; (b) $70.00-75.00; (c) $40.00-45.00.
Bottom Row: Cups and Saucers: $15.00-20.00 ea.

PLATE 68
Top Row: (a) $195.00-210.00.
Middle Row: (a) $30.00-35.00; (b) $45.00-50.00; (c) $30.00-35.00.
Bottom Row: (a) $40.00-45.00; (b) $40.00-45.00.

PLATE 69
Top Row: (a) $25.00-30.00; (b) $40.00-45.00; (c) $40.00-45.00; (d) $25.00-30.00.
Middle Row: (a) $50.00-55.00; (b) $25.00-30.00; (c) $40.00-45.00; (d) $45.00-50.00.
Bottom Row: (a) $40.00-45.00; (b) $30.00-35.00; (c) $45.00-55.00; (d) $15.00-20.00.

PLATE 70
Top Row: (a) $50.00-55.00; (b) $40.00-45.00; (c) $55.00-60.00.

Middle Row: (a) $65.00-75.00; (b) $70.00-75.00; (c) $65.00-75.00.
Bottom Row: (a) $25.00-30.00; (b) $25.00-30.00; (c) $40.00-45.00; (d) $25.00-30.00.

PLATE 71
Top Row: (a) $45.00-50.00; (b) $75.00-80.00; (c) $30.00-35.00.
Bottom Row: (a, b, d) $35.00-40.00 ea., (c) $150.00-165.00; (e) $40.00-45.00.

PLATE 72
Top Row: (a) $40.00-45.00; (b) $30.00-35.00; (c) $40.00-45.00.
Middle Row: (a) $60.00-65.00; (b) $100.00-110.00; (c) $75.00-80.00.
Bottom Row: (a, e) $40.00-45.00 ea.; (b, d) $40.00-45.00; (c) $25.00-30.00.

PLATE 73
Top Row: (a, c) $35.00-40.00; (b) $45.00-50.00.
Middle Row: (a) $25.00-30.00; (b) $25.00-30.00; (c) $25.00-30.00.
Bottom Row: (a) $25.00-30.00; (b) $40.00-45.00; (c) $25.00-30.00.

PLATE 74
Top Row: (a) $45.00-55.00; (b) $40.00-45.00; (c) $45.00-50.00.
Middle Row: (a) $50.00-55.00; (b) $35.00-40.00; (c) $40.00-45.00.
Bottom Row: (a) $65.00-70.00; (b) $25.00-30.00; (c) $20.00-25.00.

PLATE 75
Top Row: (a) $20.00-25.00; (b) $45.00-55.00; (c) $20.00-25.00.
Middle Row: (a) $60.00-65.00; (b) $45.00-50.00; (c) $25.00-30.00.
Bottom Row: (a) $35.00-40.00; (b) $30.00-35.00; (c) $20.00-25.00; (d) $30.00-35.00.

PLATE 76
Top Row: (a) $35.00-40.00; (b) $45.00-50.00; (c) $25.00-30.00.
Middle Row: (a) $45.00-50.00; (b) $50.00-55.00; (c) $165.00-175.00.
Bottom Row: (a) $25.00-35.00; (b) $30.00-35.00; (c) $25.00-35.00.

PLATE 77
Top Row: (a) $40.00-45.00; (b) $50.00-55.00; (c) $40.00-45.00; (d) $45.00-50.00.

Middle Row: (a, f) $65.00-75.00; (b, e) $10.00-12.50 set; (c) $8.50-12.50 set; (d) $15.00-20.00.
Bottom Row: (a) $55.00-60.00; (b) $45.00-50.00; (c) $60.00-70.00.

PLATE 78
Top Row: Canisters: $25.00-30.00 ea.
Middle Row: (a) $35.00-40.00; (b) $25.00-30.00; (c) $70.00-75.00; (d) $35.00-40.00.
Bottom Row: Spice Canisters: $15.00-20.00 ea.

PLATE 79
Top Row: (a) $25.00-30.00; (b) $70.00-75.00.
Bottom Row: (a, c) $55.00-60.00; (b) $55.00-60.00.

PLATE 80
$110.00-125.00 set.

PLATE 81
Top Row: (a) $70.00-75.00; (b) $75.00-80.00.
Middle Row: (a) $60.00-65.00; (b) $40.00-45.00.
Bottom Row: $50.00-55.00.

PLATE 82
Top Row: (a) $50.00-55.00; (b) $40.00-45.00; (c) $50.00-55.00.
Middle Row: (a) $55.00-60.00; (b) $55.00-60.00.
Bottom Row: (a) $40.00-45.00; (b) $30.00-35.00; (c) $35.00-40.00.

PLATE 83
Top Row: (a) $35.00-40.00; (b) $40.00-45.00; (c) $35.00-40.00.
Middle Row: (a) $30.00-35.00; (b) $35.00-40.00; (c) $30.00-35.00.
Bottom Row: (a) $30.00-35.00; (b) $40.00-45.00; (c) $30.00-35.00.

PLATE 84
Top Row: (a, c) $30.00-35.00; (b) $35.00-40.00.
Middle Row: Canisters: $15.00-20.00 ea.; Vinegar Cruet: $35.00-40.00.
Bottom Row: (a, c) $15.00-20.00; (b) $25.00-30.00.

PLATE 85
Top Row: (a) $30.00-35.00; (b) $45.00-50.00; (c) $55.00-60.00; (d) $30.00-40.00.
Middle Row: (a) $40.00-45.00; (b) $20.00-25.00; (c) $50.00-55.00; (d) $40.00-45.00; (e) $20.00-25.00.
Bottom Row: (a) $20.00-25.00; (b) $85.00-90.00; (c) $40.00-45.00.

PLATE 86
Top Row: (a) $45.00-55.00; (b) $40.00-45.00.
Middle Row: (a) $30.00-35.00; (b) $15.00-20.00.
Bottom Row: $50.00-55.00.

PLATE 87
Top Row: (a) $40.00-45.00; (b) $20.00-25.00.
Middle Row: (a) $40.00-45.00; (b) $40.00-45.00; (c) $40.00-45.00.
Bottom Row: (a) $55.00-60.00; (b) $50.00-55.00.

PLATE 88
Top Row: (a) $40.00-45.00; (b) $35.00-40.00; (c) $35.00-40.00; (d) $40.00-45.00.
Middle Row: (a) $40.00-45.00; (b) $45.00-50.00; (c) $40.00-45.00; (d) $40.00-45.00.
Bottom Row: (a) $35.00-40.00; (b) $35.00-40.00; (c) $35.00-40.00; (d) $45.00-50.00.

PLATE 89
Top Row: (a) $55.00-60.00; (b) $40.00-45.00; (c) $40.00-45.00; (d) $40.00-45.00.
Middle Row: (a) $35.00-40.00; (b) $55.00-60.00; (c) $55.00-60.00; (d) $40.00-45.00.
Bottom Row: (a) $40.00-45.00; (b) $35.00-40.00; (c) $30.00-35.00; (d) $40.00-45.00.

PLATE 90
Top Row: (a) $35.00-40.00; (b) $40.00-45.00; (c) $40.00-45.00.
Middle Row: (a) $40.00-45.00; (b) $45.00-50.00; (c) $40.00-45.00.
Bottom Row: (a) $35.00-40.00; (b) $40.00-45.00; (c) $40.00-45.00.

PLATE 91
Top Row: (a) $40.00-45.00; (b) $40.00-45.00; (c) $40.00-45.00.
Middle Row: (a) $35.00-40.00; (b) $40.00-45.00.
Bottom Row: (a) $35.00-40.00; (b) $40.00-45.00.

PLATE 92
Top Row: (a) $40.00-45.00; (b) $35.00-40.00; (c) $40.00-45.00; (d) $35.00-40.00.
Middle Row: (a) $40.00-45.00; (b) $45.00-50.00.
Bottom Row: (a) $40.00-45.00; (b) $45.00-50.00; (c) $35.00-40.00.

PLATE 93
Top Row: (a) $25.00-30.00; (b) $30.00-35.00.
Middle Row: (a) $30.00-35.00; (b) $25.00-30.00.
Bottom Row: (a) $35.00-40.00; (b) $40.00-45.00.

PLATE 94

Top Row: (a) $30.00-35.00; (b) $35.00-40.00.
Middle Row: (a) $40.00-45.00; (b) $30.00-35.00.
Bottom Row: (a) $30.00-35.00; (b) $25.00-30.00.

PLATE 95

Top Row: (a) $35.00-40.00; (b) $50.00-55.00; (c) $20.00-25.00.
Middle Row: (a) $45.00-50.00; (b) $35.00-40.00; (c) $35.00-40.00.
Bottom Row: (a) $40.00-45.00; (b) $35.00-40.00; (c) $30.00-35.00.

PLATE 96

Top Row: (a) $20.00-25.00; (b) $20.00-25.00; (c) $25.00-30.00; (d) $30.00-35.00.
Middle Row: (a) $35.00-40.00; (b) $20.00-25.00; (c) $20.00-25.00; (d) $20.00-25.00.
Bottom Row: (a) $25.00-30.00; (b) $25.00-30.00; (c) $20.00-25.00; (d) $20.00-25.00.

PLATE 97

Top Row: (a) $20.00-25.00; (b) $25.00-30.00; (c) $20.00-25.00; (d) $20.00-25.00.
Middle Row: (a) $30.00-35.00; (b) $40.00-45.00; (c) $25.00-30.00; (d) $30.00-35.00.
Bottom Row: (a) $25.00-30.00; (b) $30.00-35.00; (c) $35.00-40.00; (d) $30.00-35.00.

PLATE 98

Top Row: (a) $30.00-35.00; (b) $40.00-45.00; (c) $40.00-45.00.
Middle Row: (a) $20.00-25.00; (b) $25.00-30.00; (c) $25.00-30.00.
Bottom Row: (a) $35.00-40.00; (b) $40.00-45.00; (c) $35.00-40.00.

PLATE 99

Top Row: (a) $45.00-50.00; (b) $40.00-45.00; (c) $45.00-50.00.
Middle Row: (a) $35.00-40.00; (b) $60.00-65.00; (c) $55.00-60.00; (d) $35.00-40.00.
Bottom Row: (a) $30.00-35.00; (b) $35.00-40.00; (c) $30.00-35.00.

PLATE 100

Top Row: (a) $50.00-60.00; (b) $50.00-60.00.
Middle Row: (a) $45.00-50.00; (b) $45.00-50.00.
Bottom Row: (a) $45.00-50.00; (b) $45.00-50.00.

PLATE 101

Top Row: (a) $40.00-45.00; (b) $45.00-50.00.
Middle Row: (a) $40.00-45.00; (b) $40.00-45.00.

Bottom Row: (a) $30.00-35.00; (b) $35.00-40.00 set; (c) $35.00-40.00.

PLATE 102

Top Row: (a) $40.00-45.00; (b) $35.00-40.00; (c) $30.00-35.00.
Middle Row: (a) $40.00-45.00; (b) $40.00-45.00; (c) $40.00-45.00.
Bottom Row: (a) $55.00-60.00; (b) $40.00-45.00; (c) $35.00-40.00.

PLATE 103

Top Row: (a) $35.00-40.00; (b) $25.00-30.00; (c) $30.00-35.00.
Middle Row: (a) $35.00-40.00; (b) $55.00-60.00; (c) $35.00-40.00.
Bottom Row: (a) $35.00-40.00; (b) $30.00-35.00; (c) $35.00-40.00; (d) $35.00-40.00.

PLATE 104

Top Row: (a) $8.00-10.00; (b) $12.00-15.00; (c) $6.00-8.00.
Second Row: (a) $6.00-8.00; (b) $25.00-30.00; (c) $45.00-50.00; (d) $35.00-40.00; (e) $15.00-20.00 set.
Third Row: (a) $45.00-50.00; (b) $6.00-8.00; (c) $40.00-45.00.
Bottom Row: (a) $40.00-45.00; (b) $45.00-50.00; (c) $45.00-50.00.

PLATE 105

Top Row: (a) $10.00-12.00; (b) $60.00-65.00 set.
Middle Row: (a) $20.00-25.00; (b) $25.00-30.00.
Bottom Row: (a) $25.00-30.00; (b) $35.00-40.00; (c) $20.00-25.00.

PLATE 106

Top Row: (a) $25.00-30.00; (b) $50.00-55.00; (c) $20.00-25.00.
Bottom Row: (a) $20.00-25.00; (b) $45.00-50.00.

PLATE 107

Top Row: (a) $20.00-25.00; (b) $20.00-25.00.
Middle Row: (a) $40.00-45.00.
Bottom Row: (a) $20.00-25.00; (b) $15.00-20.00.

PLATE 108

Top Row: Mugs, set of 4: $20.00-25.00 ea.
Middle Row/Bottom Row: Mugs, set of 4: $30.00-35.00 ea.

PLATE 109

$160.00-175.00.

PLATE 110
Top Row: (a, c) $60.00-70.00; (b) $225.00-240.00.
Bottom Row: (a) $55.00-60.00; (b) $125.00-140.00;
  (c) $90.00-95.00; (d) $60.00-75.00.

PLATE 111
$65.00-70.00 ea.

PLATE 112
$155.00-160.00 ea.

PLATE 113
Top Row: Decanter: $125.00-140.00; Matching
  Glasses: $45.00-50.00 ea.
Bottom Row: (a, c) $85.00-90.00; (b) $130.00-145.00.

PLATE 114
Top Row: (a) $50.00-75.00; (b) $130.00-140.00; (c)
  $85.00-90.00.
Bottom Row: Decanter: $160.00-175.00; Matching
  Glasses: $45.00-50.00 ea.

PLATE 115
Top Row: (a) $135.00-140.00; (b) $150.00-165.00;
  (c) $145.00-150.00.
Bottom Row: (a) $75.00-85.00; (b) $180.00-200.00;
  (c) $70.00-80.00.

PLATE 116
Top Row: (a) $225.00-250.00; (b) $550.00-650.00.
Bottom Row: (a) $55.00-60.00; (b) $250.00-300.00;
  (c) $55.00-60.00.

PLATE 117
Top Row: (a, c) $30.00-35.00 ea.; (b) $40.00-45.00.
Middle Row: Decanter: $85.00-90.00; Matching
  Glasses: $30.00-35.00 ea.
Bottom Row: (a) $35.00-40.00; (b) $65.00-70.00;
  (c) $45.00-50.00.

PLATE 118
Top Row: (a) $40.00-45.00; (b) $25.00-30.00; (c)
  $35.00-40.00; (d) $30.00-35.00.
Middle Row: (a) $55.00-60.00; (b) $95.00-110.00;
  (c) $55.00-60.00.
Bottom Row: (a) $25.00-30.00; (b) $50.00-55.00;
  (c) $40.00-45.00.

PLATE 119
Crystal Glasses, set of six: $10.00-15.00 ea.

PLATE 120
Top Row: (a) $110.00-125.00; (b) $35.00-40.00 set;
  (c) $90.00-100.00.
Bottom Row: (a) $70.00-75.00; (b) $70.00-75.00.

PLATE 121
Top Row: (a) $25.00-30.00; (b) $60.00-65.00; (c)
  $25.00-30.00.
Middle Row: (a, f) $15.00-20.00 ea.; (b, e) $30.00-
  35.00 ea.; (c, d) $25.00-30.00.
Bottom Row: (a) $25.00-30.00; (b, c) $30.00-35.00
  ea.; (d) $30.00-35.00.

PLATE 122
Top Row: (a) $100.00-110.00; (b) $70.00-75.00.
Bottom Row: (a) $110.00-125.00; (b) $110.00-125.00.

PLATE 123
$80.00-85.00.

Books on Antiques and Collectibles

Most of the following books are available from your local book seller or antique dealer, or on loan from your public library. If you are unable to locate certain titles in your area you may order by mail from COLLECTOR BOOKS, P.O. Box 3009, Paducah, KY 42002-3009. Add $2.00 for postage for the first book ordered and $.30 for each additional book. Include item number, title and price when ordering. Allow 14 to 21 days for delivery. All books are well illustrated and contain current values.

Schroeder's Antiques Price Guide

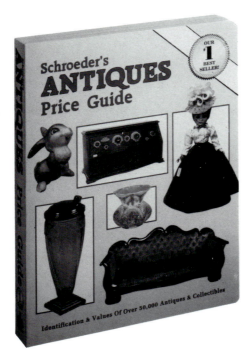

Schroeder's Antiques Price Guide has become THE household name in the antiques & collectibles field. Our team of editors works year-round with more than 200 contributors to bring you our #1 best-selling book on antiques & collectibles.

With more than 50,000 items identified & priced, Schroeder's is a must for the collector & dealer alike. If it merits the interest of today's collector, you'll find it in Schroeder's. Each subject is represented with histories and background information. In addition, hundreds of sharp original photos are used each year to illustrate not only the rare and unusual, but the everyday "fun-type" collectibles as well — not postage stamp pictures, but large close-up shots that show important details clearly.

Our editors compile a new book each year. Never do we merely change prices. Accuracy is our primary aim. Prices are gathered over the entire year previous to publication, from ads and personal contacts. Then each category is thoroughly checked to spot inconsistencies, listings that may not be entirely reflective of actual market dealings, and lines too vague to be of merit. Only the best of the lot remains for publication. You'll find Schroeder's Antiques Price Guide the one to buy for factual information and quality.

No dealer, collector or investor can afford not to own this book. It is available from your favorite bookseller or antiques dealer at the low price of $12.95. If you are unable to find this price guide in your area, it's available from Collector Books, P.O. Box 3009, Paducah, KY 42002-3009 at $12.95 plus $2.00 for postage and handling.

8½ x 11", 608 Pages   **$12.95**

COLLECTOR BOOKS
A Division of Schroeder Publishing Co., Inc.